100 BEDTIME STORIES

FOR TRIATHLETES

ALLAN PITMAN

BALBOA.
PRESS

A DIVISION OF HAY HOUSE

Balboa Press books may be ordered through booksellers or by contacting:

Balboa Press
A Division of Hay House
1663 Liberty Drive
Bloomington, IN 47403
www.balboapress.com.au
1 (877) 407-4847

Because of the dynamic nature of the Internet, any web addresses or
links contained in this book may have changed since publication and
may no longer be valid. The views expressed in this work are solely those
of the author and do not necessarily reflect the views of the publisher,
and the publisher hereby disclaims any responsibility for them.

The author of this book does not dispense medical advice or prescribe the use
of any technique as a form of treatment for physical, emotional, or medical
problems without the advice of a physician, either directly or indirectly. The
intent of the author is only to offer information of a general nature to help
you in your quest for emotional and spiritual well-being. In the event you use
any of the information in this book for yourself, which is your constitutional
right, the author and the publisher assume no responsibility for your actions.

Artwork by Brett Travis of Travis Creative

Print information available on the last page.

ISBN: 978-1-5043-0651-5 (sc)
ISBN: 978-1-5043-0652-2 (e)

Balboa Press rev. date: 02/23/2017

One Hundred Bedtime Stories for Triathletes is as gripping, motivating, and insightful as you would expect to get from a book full of stories based around triathlons, a sport that attracts those who want more excitement, more challenges, and more experience in their lives.

Swimming, riding, and running, in that order without a break between (well technically you can take a break, but you can't leave the race course!), is an adrenaline rush no matter what the distances. But a 3.8 kilometre swim and 180 kilometre ride, followed by a 42.2 kilometre run (marathon). takes more than adrenaline and a pair of swim costumes. Those distances make up an Ironman triathlon, and the Ironman World Championship is held in Hawaii each year; hence, the pinnacle of the sport being the Hawaii Ironman. It is hallowed ground, where only the fittest, toughest athletes dare to set foot on the start line. Getting there is a long, hard road of qualification and many, many hours of dedicated training that requires commitment both physically and mentally. The phrase "It is the journey, not the destination that matters" is never truer than when describing the goal of being on the start line of an Ironman, ready to give your all to the next 226 kilometres. If you are not ready to do your best, no matter what unknown obstacles the day may throw at you and no matter how fast or slow you go, the finish line will mean little. Within these pages, you will read accounts of the many paths that journey may lead toward, the trials and errors you may avoid, and directions on how to get the most out of your journey—all documented here over many years by Allan Pitman.

I can't remember when I met Al, but it was a long time ago, through a mutual friend, Bruce, who trained in his Cycos tri-squad. We hit it off, as we both like being (and urge to be) creative, and landscaping is our major outlet for that, as well as our ability to listen to our instincts. Bruce could see that I was talented, that I was following a goal to win Hawaii, and that I was doing it on my own without much direction. He generously sponsored me through his company, and part of that arrangement was that Al would become my mentor and coach toward my goals. And so it followed.

In the years leading to my World Championship win in 2012, Allan guided me physically and trained me mentally. That helped me to visualise, build confidence, hone focus, improve efficiency, and ready myself so that race day would have no surprises that I couldn't deal with in a calm and controlled way to provide the best outcome. On race day, I was off the bike in second place, over eight minutes behind the leader, but still I stopped to stretch my hips after five kilometres, as I knew that would release the pain in my lower back and lead to an overall faster run. The training sessions in race conditions had allowed me to remain patient, remain calm, and do exactly as I had practiced for the best outcome, while to onlookers it appeared as though I was in trouble. The reality was that I was going through the motions of a perfect dress rehearsal without the pressure of opening night.

Knowing who you are and why you are doing something makes it more worthwhile. And if you meet Al, you'll find out pretty quick who you are, because he'll tell you. Not one to dance around the point, Al has a harsh but fair approach to encouraging people to question themselves, by throwing wild curveballs they never expected someone would throw at them. Such unexpected assaults make most learn quickly to toughen up, build character, become smarter, become more self-aware, and improve their situations. And that's why Al says he genuinely wants everyone to try to improve. Whether it be advice on triathlon training, relationships, or career, Al's reputation as "The Counsellor" is infamous among his squad that has become an incredibly successful unit of well-balanced individuals in all aspects of life. His influence reaches deep into people's subconscious, and his own memory is even deeper for the countless books, stories, and experiences he has accumulated since the day he was born. All add to his bank of advice, which, like it or not, is coming your way.

Enjoy!
Pete Jacobs

WORK WITH THEM;
THEY'RE YOUR BIGGEST ASSETS

· · · • ◉ • · · ·

Winter is the time of year when we can creep forward, always gaining a little bit. You don't have to kill yourself in training in the colder months to gain. They say summer's races are won in winter. Every one is going to struggle a little bit getting out of bed when it's cold and dark outside. It's the time of day when the strength of your goals is tested.

It's times like this when our training partners, our mates, are our biggest assets. Having a commitment to meet someone is one of the best tools to have in our toolboxes. Many of us can let ourselves down by taking the easy option, but most of us will not let our mates down. The thought of our training mates waiting out in the cold, dark morning is often enough to force us to make the move.

I have to admit that in thirty years of Ironman (IM) training, I have had periods of low motivation. I have used commitments to meeting people to get me out of bed on many occasions. It's always easier when spring comes and the days are longer, but the steady work done in winter gives you a better platform on which to build your new season.

Right now I am fourteen weeks out from Hawaii Ironman. I know that my main training includes the ten to twelve weeks leading into the race. I also know how fast the last ten weeks seems to go. At fourteen weeks, it seems an awfully long time until I need to be fit, but I also know that the consistency built through winter is a huge asset to take into the final ten weeks.

At my age and my stage of development, training for my forty-second Ironman, I have different training needs from my developing athletes. But my developing athletes will probably be gaining more than I can hope to gain by being super consistent through winter. A developing athlete needs to focus on accumulating training hours while honing skills in each sport. It takes many hours to develop an endurance athlete to his or her potential.

I encourage each one of you to put pressure on your training mates when they don't show up. You'll be helping them, and you'll be giving them ammunition to use against you if you don't make it one day. This is a good thing.

The biggest asset you can have in your development is a training partner who is driven to be the best he or she can be.

Eagles don't fly with pigeons.

KNOWLEDGE VERSUS WISDOM

· · · • ◉ • · · ·

In 2007 I spent a week at the Super Sports Centre at Runaway Bay on the Gold Coast, doing the opening leg of the level-three triathlon coach's course.

To be honest, I only applied for selection (only ten coaches of elite athletes from around Australia were selected) to spend time with the best coaches and share ideas. To me, being level three is a bit hollow. My goal is to be the best triathlon coach I can possibly be. When I have one of my athletes standing on the podium, whether it's at the Hawaii Ironman or the local enticer series, it doesn't matter too much what level I am.

It was an excellent experience facilitated by Bill Daveron and Craig Redmond of Triathlon Australia (TA). The format was, apart from four presenters (all experts in their fields), group discussion and problem solving. It was a workshop-type atmosphere.

In the past, when I had been to coaching seminars or at the level two course, I was with much the same group of coaches.

At previous gatherings, I felt like a bit of an outsider. Many of the other coaches had sports-science backgrounds. My own background is based on the study of sports science from a background of experience. I have raced over thirty Ironman competitions, coming from the back of the field to gradually working my way up to place as an age grouper several times in Hawaii.

Some of the other coaches have never raced a triathlon but have enough degrees and diplomas to wallpaper my office.

I've felt like an outsider because I have always believed coaching is 70 per cent intuition, reading body language, and people skills and 30 per cent sports science.

The rest of the group approaches the task from a perspective of 90 per cent sports science and 10 per cent people skills.

I just couldn't see it that way. We're dealing with people who have doubts, fears, ambitions, passions, and a good old bit of mongrel in them. Now, it doesn't matter how much physical talent an athlete has; he or she is still a person and needs to be approached from the human angle. It's not like programming a robot.

But like in the movies, this story has a happy ending.

Now that these coaches have reached the level of "elite coaches," they unanimously agree that coaching is 70 per cent people skills and 30 per cent sports science.

I'm so happy for them. How could they have reached their coaching potential with the old view?

An arrow can only be shot by pulling it backward. So when life is dragging you back with difficulties, it means it's going to launch you into something great. So just focus and keep aiming.

A DAY IN THE LIFE OF A CHAMPION

For the past two weeks, Pete Jacobs has stayed at our house in order to train with the Cycos squad on our Walloon time-trial course. The best way to test your feeding strategy and equipment is in time trials. On Sunday, the twenty-third, three weeks out from Kona, we did a 150-kilometre time trial (TT) followed by five, one-kilometre repeats on the run course. My own Saturday was spent tiling the laundry at home, after coaching the morning swim squad and having a swim myself. I worked to 5:00 p.m. and really didn't eat that well—and I definitely should have drunk more.

On Sunday, I paid for my lack of preparation. You can get away with one hundred kilometres on poor preparation

(I have many times), but a 150-kilometre TT puts you into a situation much closer to an Ironman bike. There's nowhere to hide in the last fifty kilometres. Our course is around 16.5 kilometres per lap. One hundred fifty kilometres is nine laps from the roundabout in Walloon to the roundabout in Rosewood and back, both quiet, little country towns about a forty-minute drive west of Brisbane. The course is undulating, not unlike the Hawaii Ironman course.

Pete is in fantastic shape. He's prepared well with the Hawaii Ironman as his number-one race this season. His second place last year was no fluke. Five years ago, we set the goal of winning Hawaii as a five-year plan. He's had three top-ten places now. This is his eighth year as a pro triathlete. It hasn't been an easy career path to follow. A lot of guys his age have been earning a lot more money over those seven years. But success in life is more about aiming high, overcoming lots of setbacks along the way, and never taking your eyes off your target. In the end, it's a lot more satisfying than settling into a job that is not fulfilling but pays the bills.

Pete has had his fair share of setbacks, including minor injuries and illnesses that would have caused a less motivated athlete to drop by the wayside. He has his dreams and is surrounded by a great support network. His wife, Jaimie; his parents, Jen and Geoff; and his extended family are all in Kona each year as Team Jacobs. I personally find that the closer your relationship with your supporters, the harder it is to let them down. At some time in that race, we all switch from being driven to achieve our dreams to being driven by the feeling of letting ourselves and our supporters down. There is a switch that happens for everyone out there, from the desire to win to the fear of losing. You have to be ready for that moment.

On Sunday, the twenty-third, I struggled. I went through one hundred kilometres in 3:09 and faded through the last fifty kilometres to end up averaging around thirty-two kilometres per hour. As I tried to get off my bike, I cramped and fell on the ground. I managed to run one of my planned one-kilometre repeats before throwing the towel in. Pete smashed the 150 kilometres, making it look like he was taking it easy all the way. He averaged forty-one kilometres per hour and then got off and ran so fast that the other guys just watched in awe. I vowed to prepare better next weekend.

On Saturday, the twenty-ninth, we started the day with the Cycos stretching session. If we didn't do the group-stretching session each week, I'm sure many would never find time to stretch. This is followed by our core-strength segment. Again, I'm sure if we didn't do core-strength work as a group three times a week, many would find something else to do with that time. Then it's on to the swim squad. We had several time trials in the 3,500-metre session. Pete was not swimming at his best. We did a one-hour Bikram

Yoga session the evening before, and it really affected training the next morning.

After swim squad, the Cycos monthly free breakfast was served to all members. Volunteers Meredith and Anna prepare all the food, and the club covers the costs. This is one of the things that makes our club special. If there's anything worth discussing, this becomes a club meeting. We have a different pair of volunteers for each monthly breakfast. I had a swim right after the squad while the guys were grazing on the breakfast banquet. After breakfast, Pete and I headed out to meet our kinesiologist, Ian Maitland. I have been working with Ian for fourteen years, and over the past five years, Pete has flown up from Sydney several times to see him.

Our meeting with Ian is an important move in being totally ready for a major race. He is able to test for nutritional deficiencies and important mental preparation issues. It's the little things that make the difference. A champion only has to be 1 per cent off his game, and another competitor takes advantage. The 1 per cents are made up of core strength, flexibility, perfect refuelling after workouts, and the right nutrition in the overall diet. Anyone who says athletes don't need food supplements just does not know what they're talking about.

After a really productive session with Ian, Pete and I visited a discount chemist shop for the "right brand of

BCAAs," went across to Ada St Body Building su[p] the "right brand of Q10," and then had lunch. Mex[i] with extra servings of rice. When we got home, I made a rice pudding. This week instead of tiling, I laid down for a sleep. Pete set his alarm, but I just slept as long as I needed. I'd had a couple of late nights and obviously needed the sleep. Pete slept for ninety minutes and got up for a light forty-minute run. I woke up after two and a half hours. An afternoon snack of fresh home-made rice pudding topped up the glycogen stores.

We watched a bit of sport on TV while we waited for dinner. Pete does a bit of extra stretching while he watches TV. Some genius has said good runners don't need to stretch, but don't believe everything some anonymous expert posts on a triathlon forum. Pete has posted the fastest run in the Hawaii Ironman for the past two years. Sandy is a great cook and enjoys entertaining. Today she's cooked peri-peri chicken with green veges and more rice. I've found the rice-based carbo loading to be most effective, but once again, I have been challenged on this by yet another "expert" on a forum. A couple of years ago, Susan Casey and Sandy were racing IMNZ. I was their coach/cook for the days leading into the race. I loaded them up with rice-based dishes. They won their categories by forty-five and fifty-five minutes. There was a search party out looking for their competitors.

ıg, I had my normal double espresso at ıe way to Walloon. We did have perfect ɔnditions. Pete ripped out a two-hour, nute, one hundred kilometre. That's an of 42.5 kilometres per hour. He ran his one-kɪ _ ɔeats fast, with a five hundred-metre recovery at a four-minute pace. He looks ready. I rode the fastest one hundred kilometre I had ridden in ten years. I rode it in two hours and fifty-two minutes—34.8 kilometres per hour. I ran my planned five, one kilometres, leaving on five minutes. I felt so good doing it that I added a shirtless extra one kilometre for laughs.

Proper preparation prevents poor performances—we looked forward to the following weekend's training in Kona.

I'm too positive to be doubtful, too optimistic to be fearful, and too determined to be defeated.

Are You Going for a Pass or Excellence?

I'm always amused by students who rejoice at managing a pass in their exams. They celebrate as though they've won the lottery. Whatever happened to shooting high? I read a report that told the story of a bunch of teenagers who were asked what they wanted most. Their answer was to be famous. Not famous for doing something particularly well, just famous.

Lots of us limit our outcomes by shooting too low. Is it because we're not game to aim high, in case we fail? If we did choose excellence, instead of just a pass, how would we go about achieving it?

The first step is to value ourselves enough to feel worthy of achieving excellence. To start that process, we have to become good at accepting compliments and recording little wins. Lots of little wins will build confidence. An increase in confidence will allow bigger dreams, higher goals.

Once the higher goals are chosen, an attitude of seeking excellence in everything we do must be adopted. Success always comes back to the little things being done very well.

These basic principles can easily be adapted to our sport. Start by keeping a diary and recording what went right in every workout. Record time trial and race results. Next step is to have clear achievable goals set for the next month or over the next three months. These short-term goals are more important than the long-term, three-year or five-year plan, because it's the little wins along the way that provide the fuel to keep going.

Paying attention to the small things that many overlook will pay off in the long run. The greatest gains in our sport often don't come from training. They can come from body maintenance: stretching, strengthening, and resting—regularly taking a simple day off to refresh the body and mind.

If at first you don't succeed, try doing what your coach told you to do the first time.

Do Your Goals Give You Goose Bumps?

I meet lots of people who have goals.

When someone tells me his or her goals, whether they're race goals or general life goals, I can tell if it's just talk or if that person is going to make them happen.

It seems that when you speak about your goals, if you believe what you're saying can actually happen, your body language changes.

If the goal is truly inspiring and if it raises your level of passion, then what you feel on the inside shows on the outside. Passionate people perform.

When I sign up a new athlete or when an established athlete starts a new season, I ask them to give me their goals for that season. I want them to be fairly specific.

Usually this process is to get them to talk about them or write about them. At least this starts them thinking about them. I want my athletes to be driven by their desire to reach their goals.

Whether you're Tiger Woods, Lance Armstrong, Casey Stoner, or Chris McCormack, the amount of passion connected to your goal is the power that drives you.

If you think you have a goal, learn to sight it regularly. Turn on the vision when the alarm clock goes off early in the morning. Turn it on when you come home from work and you're due to start a workout before dinner.

If sighting that goal doesn't excite you, it may be time to look into the goal more closely. The true test of the strength of your goal is when conditions are not ideal. Any fool can train when he or she feels good. Champions can get something out of every session.

If you can use your goals to get you through really tough training sessions, you've tested them. Those goals will get you through tough race situations.

Stand up for something, even if it means standing alone. Because often, the one who flies alone has the strongest wings.

Goal Setting—No Options Available

When I start a new athlete on a training plan, I want a short-term goal, a mid-term goal, and a three-to-five-year goal. I also often ask for a career goal, a relationship goal, and sporting goals. All of these things influence each other. You really can't be directionless in two-thirds of your life and totally committed in the other third.

Balance is so very important in order to reach your total potential. Coaches become good at reading body language. Everyone unconsciously reads body language all of the time, but coaches hone these skills through practice. When someone states his or her goals to me in person, it's usually pretty obvious whether the goals are coming from the heart or whether it's just a mouth talking.

I once asked Kieren Perkins, a great distance swimmer, "What do you get out of bed for on dark, cold mornings, to go training, when you already have two Olympic gold medals? You hold the world record, and you're the fastest man in the world over fifteen hundred metres in the pool."

He said, "When I started swimming, I wanted three Olympic gold medals, and I only have two." When Kieren spoke, it came from the heart. There was no doubt in his voice or his body language. He knew what he wanted. He went on to the next Olympics and nearly pulled it off; he came home with silver.

We all have goals. We can evaluate how strong our goals are by how many options we give ourselves. Like Kieren, what if when that alarm goes off in the morning, you just get up. No thinking, no consideration of any other option. The alarm is set for a reason; it's time to get up and move forward toward your goals. Lying there and running other possible options through your mind indicates that your goal is not strong enough.

Now, if your goal is not strong enough at that critical moment, you will consider taking the easy option on race day. The sort of races we train for force us into positions where we're pushed to the limits. It's at these points where the strength of our goals will be tested. There are no options when it comes to doing the right thing—being true to ourselves.

Most people don't realise that the strength of their goals is being tested every day. For those who need to shed a bit of extra weight to perform without excuses, the strength of their goals is tested every time they're tempted to snack. Being aware is good, but awareness alone won't get you to where you want to be. You have to know what you want, really want. You have to own that goal so strongly that there are no options.

You can do it.

If You Really Want It, Get Serious Now

A year is divided into sections for our squad members. When they complete a section, they reset their goals.

Over the years, the Gold Coast Marathon is one of those resetting points. Even people who don't do the marathon reset their goals about that time.

The next reset time seems to be the start of November, when Kona Ironman and Noose triathlon weekend are both over. The first of January is also a significant date for some.

If you have just completed Kona or Noosa and are thinking about your future, immediately following your reality check in your recent race, you need to be clear with your goals.

Unless you're very new in the sport, it's pretty hard to advance all three disciplines at once. Usually the leg you need to improve most needs special attention while maintaining the other two legs of the sport. Be clear with what you want. You can't have everything, and some things take more time than others.

When you know what you want, talk to me about it. Let's make a plan. You will never reach great heights without first digging good foundations.

Even though many of us have had great performances when viewed by others, we are never truly satisfied with our results. That's the addictive part about this sport.

If we're totally honest with ourselves (and we must be to be the best we can be) we can find some things we could have done better in our preparation. Little things on our plans we left out or did half-heartedly. Moving forward, are we going to do all these little things better?

I'm talking about the "bike to pool and home" that was left out, the "arrive late and skip half the core work," or the "run that was meant to be done right after the swim that was either left out or done half-heartedly later in the day." These are just a few of the little things where we cut corners.

Well, let me tell you. The people who kicked your ass probably didn't discount as much as you did. They're the ones who turned up when they were tired. The coach modified their session a little, but they were there, not in bed.

Those ripped people you saw on race day are probably not the same ones you saw hitting the beer and pizzas. They're probably the ones who took the long way around the cookie jar at work. In fact, they probably looked the other way as they passed the cookie jar.

Early November is as good a time as any to ask yourself, how serious am I about these goals? Are they really goals, or are they just day dreams?

Passionate people perform.

The Long-Term Plan

You have been shaped by all your past experiences. The person looking back at you from the mirror has been transformed from the fresh young kid you once were into what you see now. Every experience has shaped the way you relate to other people, the way you approach difficulties, and the attitude you have.

Your mind has been shaped by people you've met over the years, and every skill you have today had to be learned. You've been shaping yourself from when you were a child. It's not someone else shaping you; you have individual responsibility to build the future you want for yourself.

Many of us have come into this sport as adults. We wish we had started swimming when we were ten years old, but it's too late to go back, unless we have access to Doctor Who's Tardis. We can't change much of what has happened up to now, but we can always improve what we have in skills. We do get to an age where it's not possible to become aerobically fitter or very much stronger, but we can always be working on being more efficient with what we have.

I found that my own physical peak happened at around fifty-one years. That year I achieved my best placing in Hawaii and ran my fastest Ironman marathon. That was the product of the previous six years of working on aerobic efficiency and improved technique. I had been to a seminar run by Phil Maffetone in Hawaii in '93. Also that year, I had started working with Greg Menz, who taught The Alexander Technique (a process of refining all movements and posture).

During those six years of aerobic development, I ran the Gold Coast marathon on three consecutive years, simply as training for Ironman. I ran exactly the same time each year (without wearing a watch) but ran at five heart-rate beats lower each year. I was running the same pace at a heart rate ten beats lower than three years earlier.

I had gone from having to walk over minor hills to keep my heart rate below 153 beats per minute to being able to run over Mount Cootha at below 140 beats per minute.

So the message is never stop working on improving technique and efficiency in each sport. Don't worry about what pace others are training at. The guys who used to laugh at me restricting my heart rate and letting them run away from me are no longer in the game. They've dropped by the wayside for one or more reasons.

Have a long-term plan. It's a little like investing. The investment experts say most people overestimate what they can save in one year and underestimate what they can save over ten years. Endurance sport is just the same.

I have seen lots of young guys give the game away when they were so close to breaking through. Then I've seen lots of less talented athletes reach great heights by simply sticking to the plan.

In endurance sport, a long-term plan will pay off.

Holding a grudge doesn't make you stronger; it makes you bitter. Forgiving doesn't make you weak; it sets you free.

Finishing Things Off

For years I've been politely suggesting to athletes in my squad that they run 401 metres when they're running 400 metre efforts on the track. Not 398 metres, as a lot like to do, slowing down over the last few metres. Same thing in the pool; I want fifty metres, not forty-eight metres and a walk into the end.

This may sound petty to some, but there is a strong psychological reason for completing what you start. It's the difference to walking twenty steps through each aid station in an Ironman compared to running all the way. It works out to approximately ten to twelve minutes over the marathon. But it's worse than that; it's giving in. It's going soft on yourself. It's choosing to be soft/easy on yourself for very little gain. It doesn't hurt any more to jog through an aid station than it takes to walk a bit. On the track, it doesn't save the hurt one bit to start slowing down before the line. It does show a big crack in your psychological preparation for your next race.

I read *Don't Die with the Music in You*, the story of Wayne Bennett, one of the greatest rugby league coaches to walk on this planet. In the first five pages, I came across what the author described as Wayne's greatest annoyance—his players slowing down before they had finished a fast effort. Running forty-eight metres instead of fifty metres. I had to smile to myself; athletes will take the easy way if you don't keep your eyes on them.

Another area where athletes of all sports can gain a lot is in finishing off rehabilitation after an injury.

Too many athletes don't do the little things to prevent injury. Core-strength work; stretching; refuelling well; getting good hours of sleep; and having massage, acupuncture, and chiropractic adjustments. Yet when they become injured, they bleat like lost sheep. Why me? Poor me; I'll never get over this. I'll never be ready for my race in time. Why me?

The next step, the athlete is prepared to spend whatever it takes to get right. They'll take anything they can get their hands on to help them get better faster. They'll put the physio's kids through private school with the number of visits they make. They'll try every alternate therapy known to man, they'll take herbs, and they'll do anything to get back into training.

Once the symptoms have gone, they're so happy to get back into training right where they left off. It's often hard to hold them back for a week or two so that they gradually take up the load.

Then this is where many make their biggest mistake.

When the symptoms have gone, it doesn't mean the injury has totally healed or the muscle imbalance has been totally righted. It just means that the athlete is almost right.

Almost right is not going to handle a full workload. Almost right is the same as almost broken.

The reason the athlete has become injured is usually because of a weakness. The weakness may be lack of flexibility. It may be lack of core strength. It may be poor technique or a combination of all three.

Finish the treatment off. Band-Aid repairs don't last. Follow the treatment through until the flexibility, strength, or technique have been fully addressed. Even if you don't consider the time losses and the setback in athlete development, consider the costs. Have you ever met a physio whose kids did not go to a private school?

Everything happens for a reason. Sometimes the reason is you're stupid and make bad decisions.

Training to Race or Racing to Train?

This is a subject I have covered many times in newsletter articles. I have to revisit it about every six months. Usually when we get a few new squad members who just don't get it.

Endurance training is best done at a pace that stimulates the development of the athlete's fat-burning system. This pace is fairly easy. Lots of hours at 50- to 70-per cent heart rate. Training at this pace usually means that when the workout is over, the athlete can take the kids and dog for a walk, mow the lawn, or vacuum the carpets.

It should not leave you flogged. You shouldn't be so wiped out by the workout that you have to flop onto your bed. If an endurance workout leaves you feeling totally wasted, you're either dehydrated, doing it too hard, or not refuelling well enough after previous workouts.

Going too hard: If the object is to build the biggest endurance base, the answer is to do as much endurance training as you can possibly recover from. If you do endurance training at the right pace, it's easy, it doesn't wear you out, and you can get more of it done. There has to be a good reason why we see groups of A-grade cyclists and pro cyclists spinning along, talking to each other at high cadence, and out late in the mornings. They've been out for three, maybe four hours, spinning away, practicing perfect technique.

If those very good cyclists spend so many hours riding easy, why do we see beginner cyclists and mediocre triathletes racing each other and anyone who dares show up on the road in front of them?

Those very good cyclists we see doing their endurance work at such an easy pace do go hard sometimes. They go very hard, but not during an endurance session.

The biggest mistake I've seen self-trained, age-group triathletes make is to do the endurance training too hard and be too wrecked to put any effort into their hard stuff. As a result, they never extend their endurance base as far as they could, because they get too tired and become run down before they reach their goals. And they're unable to put the effort into A/T, VO2 max, or lactic tolerance workouts because they're never fresh enough. As a result, they improve up to a point where their progress grinds to a halt.

You will improve no matter what you do, as long as you're out there doing it. But this type of approach is only good for a year or so. After that, you just keep trying like a fly trying to get through a closed window, and you go nowhere.

Ongoing improvement over several years is what is going to take an athlete to his or her potential. A triathlete will never reach potential in one or two seasons. So a long-term plan must involve blocks of pure endurance building. After all, the shortest triathlon anyone will ever do is still an endurance event. They call short triathlons *sprints*, yet the fastest people take more than thirty minutes to complete them.

A sprint in any other sport takes fewer than thirty seconds. In any other sport, an event that takes thirty minutes is an endurance event and treated as such in training.

As triathletes, we have to train for long-term development, never lose sight of the fact we are endurance athletes, and train in a way that will have improved performances season after season.

Worry is a waste of time; it achieves nothing and robs you of your happiness.

Training Like a Pro

I was reading our Tara's report on the Triathlon Ireland site. She was talking about how much she'd enjoyed the time recently when Pete Jacobs spent a couple of weeks training in the squad in preparation for the New Zealand Ironman on the first of March.

She was surprised to see how similar her training was to Pete's program.

What she hadn't realised was that for the previous year, she had been training like a pro. Our age groupers train like professional athletes. They have to fit it in around their jobs, but their training is remarkably similar to what a pro athlete does.

All of the members of our squad are overachievers. They all have responsible jobs and are leaders in their fields. They are all very good at time management. They have to be.

Lots of age-group triathletes have the impression that pro athletes do enormous mileages in training. The triathlon magazines are to blame for this. I often have had to battle with age groupers who believe they should try to emulate the distances talked about in stories, written by journalists about pro triathletes.

One of the main differences between a pro athlete and an age grouper is recovery time. That recovery time allows an athlete to bounce back a little better after each workout and often fit in another session. All of my athletes have a professional attitude to diet, training, and racing nutrition.

Another area age groupers can be more professional is developing core strength and flexibility. In our squad sessions, I include one, thirty-minute stretching session each week and three short but specific core-strength sessions. It's up to individual athletes to use what they learn here to improve on their weaknesses.

I am amazed at how some of my squad members who have lofty goals don't seriously work at improving their flexibility. You know who you are. Do something about it.

What Tara has not realised is I am training her as a professional athlete. I have been training her that way for most of her time with me. After I realised her talent level and we spoke about her goals, I felt it was inevitable she would step across to the professional ranks once she achieved her Hawaii, age-group goals.

That gave us a year to prepare her for a smooth transition.

It takes years to develop an athlete to his or her potential. Along that journey, the athlete and the coach learn a lot about each other. We might as well do everything as well as it can be done.

There is only one road to human greatness.
It's through the school of hard knocks.

Ten Thousand Hours to Make a Champion

At a recent level-three coaches course (the final segment in the saga), one of the guest speakers spoke of the universally accepted view amongst coaches—that it takes ten thousand hours for an athlete in any sport to win an Olympic Gold Medal. It appears it's the same amount of development needed for a cyclist to reach the Tour de France. Since I've been on holidays, I've been reading books, lots of books. The ten thousand-hour theory applies to business leaders as well.

The widely held view is that to reach the top of any field, it generally takes ten thousand hours of deliberate practice, not just fooling around with your mates at the pool or cruising around on your BMX.

I've always told athletes in the squad that it takes seven years to develop an aerobic system to its potential. So be patient; you're a work in progress.

One of the most frustrating parts of being a coach of age-group athletes training for Ironman races is that after a season preparing for a major race and gaining significantly over the twelve to sixteen weeks, some athletes take a recovery break and don't come back for six months. They lose the opportunity for ongoing development and the chance to start the next preparation at a higher level.

If work commitments or family responsibilities cause you to stay away from the group, have a plan of action in place to continue working on some of the parts of your performance. It can be a period of strength work in the gym or it can be three short technique-based swim sessions each week, where small changes in stroke are gradually introduced.

I know some athletes who have surprised themselves at the heights they have reached by simply sticking at it for long enough.

Some interesting things come out when a group of coaches get together.

1. There are no secrets to success; it's all about doing the work. Doing it as wisely as possible but still doing it.

2. Success at high levels in sport is mostly mental; everybody will arrive at the start line in great shape

3. You have to know where you're going. Have an end in mind.

4. Keep records. Do you have a personal best (PB) book? Do you know what you ate during that great weekend when you were at your best?

Stay happy; don't waste energy of things you cannot change.

Inner Health

A bottle of probiotics belongs in every athlete's fridge.

Last year in Kona, Norman Stadler and Faris Al-Sultan both said a stomach bug was the reason for their failure to finish and failure to start the Hawaii Ironman.

I recommend every athlete take a probiotic like Health World's Inner Health each day in the week or two leading into a major race. Use it as an insurance policy against stomach upsets.

Anyone travelling to a foreign country should carry a probiotic, just in case.

There is a balance in our stomachs between the good bacteria and the bad bacteria. They're constantly waging war on each other. When you take antibiotics, excess alcohol, or other medications, you lower the number of good and bad bacteria in your stomach. If the "bad guys" multiply too quickly, or if you eat or drink something contaminated, the bad guys can get the upper hand, and you can become sick.

Avoiding a situation like that in the very important days leading into the race can be as simple as taking Inner Health.

Every athlete's fridge should have a bottle.

If something goes wrong, whether it's in training, racing, or life, the faster you can turn the page and get on with things, the less you're going to be held up.

The Male Ego—Friend or Foe

Why is it that girls respond more to coaching in triathlons than guys do?

It seems that guys follow coaching plans fairly well until they achieve a certain level. Then once they make it or achieve a level where they get respect from their peers, their egos become bigger than their brains. Very often, then, when they would benefit most from coaching, they take over the role themselves.

The easiest part of developing an athlete is the first year or two. His body responds to the work quickly and easily. Good results and PBs flow out of every race.

Once the easy results have been gained, the athlete needs to work on very specific parts of his performance—put in a lot of work for a smaller rate of improvement. Breakthroughs don't come in every race. Reducing an athlete's ten-kilometre run time from thirty-six minutes to thirty-three minutes can take three years of work. That's why there are not many thirty-three minute runners out there. But to reduce his ten-kilometre time from forty-eight minutes to forty minutes may only take three or four months.

Girls have a less distorted view of their abilities than young guys do. They're more in touch with reality. I guess it's the testosterone. Guys with lots of testosterone are the ones who jump motorcycles over busses and go base jumping. Girls don't do that sort of thing too often.

Frequently, young male athletes allow their egos to stand between them and their coaches. If a close, trusting relationship is able to be cultivated, great results will follow as they work together as partners.

We need a big ego to support great expectations and to achieve great things. But that ego needs to be under control. Don't let it stand in your way or cause you to make short-term decisions. A long-term view and a plan to support it is what you need to achieve your dreams.

I'm sure it's because of this reason that I have had more success in coaching female athletes than males. The girls are more patient and have a more conscientious attitude to details.

It's very frustrating for a coach to get a guy up to base level where he can work with him to go from good to great, and then he goes off for three months of boozing and womanising. Now, I want it on the record that I'm not against boozing and womanising. In fact, I'm a staunch advocate of the practice. But I really would like to schedule it into the program in measured amounts at strategic times of the year to not interfere with the development of the aerobic animal.

**All winners are risk takers; not all
risk takers are winners.**

Pressure Is a Privilege

We have all felt the pressure to perform at some time. Most of the time we put that pressure on ourselves. Often the pressure we put on ourselves is a result of our own high standards. If we consistently perform to a high standard in other areas of our lives, we naturally expect to give our best on race day. A glance around our squad will show that they're all overachievers.

The other day I had a phone conversation with one of our Hawaii qualifiers. She had an upcoming race in Kona in four weeks. We discussed how she saw the day unfolding. She was very excited about the whole experience. This was her first Hawaii Ironman. She talked about the pressure she put on herself to perform and how that would affect her.

She quoted a very good affirmation. "Pressure is a privilege" if you spend your life performing to a high standard in every area of your life. Hawaii qualifiers have already proven that they belong in this group. People get used to you performing well in every situation in your life. It's not unusual for friends and work colleagues to say things that suggest they expect big things from you. I've heard interviews with Hawaii Ironman winners stating that the year after the first win is the most difficult year to race because of the media and public expectation—the pressure to perform.

Now, when you look at the affirmation "Pressure is a privilege," the pressure to perform is a privilege you have earned by being a performer. Do this little exercise to help put that pressure in balance.

Draw a big, high ladder with a diving board on top and a small pool at the bottom. Draw yourself at the top of that diving board about to dive into the little pool. Now draw an audience of stick people, each one representing one of your supporters. Each one of these supporters expects you to make the right decisions at the right times. They expect you to be tough under pressure because you always have been. Now if you list all of your fears and doubts above your little stick figure, all of your supporters know that none of these things are going to be an issue, because you always overcome these things.

So here you are, the hero of all these supporters, doubting yourself, when all of your family and friends know you'll do the right thing. I have used this little exercise to totally wash away my fears and doubts.

Don't fear change; change is inevitable. Be ready to go with it; be ready to adapt.

How Many Rivets Could You Leave Out?

Today I was walking my dogs on our standard Monday morning walk, across the cycle bridge, under the train-line underpass to the little coffee shop. They patiently sit while I have a coffee, read the paper, and chat to the regulars. And then we walk home. They have lots of friends who say hello to them and give them a pat. This is the highlight of their day.

As we crossed the cycle bridge over the river, we walked alongside the railway bridge. It's a fifty-year-old steel structure held together with thousands of rivets. I looked at it and wondered how many rivets could be left out and the bridge still be strong enough to carry the heavy-goods trains? It could certainly hold up if a few were missing. In fact, I'm sure someone could go through the bridge and remove 20 per cent of the rivets without the bridge failing when a heavy train went across. But this would put more stress on the remaining rivets, more than the designers would want.

The engineers have obviously designed the bridge to hold up under much greater loads than would ever be placed on it. Engineers do that. They won't sign off on a job that has not been done to the plan.

I started thinking about a typical Ironman preparation, where many small things make a difference. A very small difference. But grouped together, they make an athlete's structures so strong that they are unbreakable under pressure. Every vitamin tablet, every hour of sleep, and every stretch plays a part in creating the unbreakable athlete.

This could even be broken down to every thought having some effect on the athlete's confidence on race day. If every doubt is washed away by a reassuring affirmation, its negative impact is neutralized. This is a good argument for avoiding negative people and seeking out the company of motivated people who encourage excellence.

So back to the "rivets in the bridge" theory. How many stretching sessions could you afford to leave out? How many times could you train without refuelling well right after? How many swim sessions could you miss before it cost you some performance on race day?

If every rivet does a small job in making the bridge unbreakable, then every fish-oil capsule has a role to play in your A race of the season. If we had an engineer inspecting every part of our training, recovery, and body maintenance program, would he sign off on the way we've put the job together?

Do you want to stand at the start line, feeling unbreakable? The alternative is to race with your fingers crossed, hoping nothing goes wrong. If we took 20 per cent of the rivets out of the bridge, the engineer would have trouble sleeping when the big freight trains came through.

Race with your team, your club members. Encourage them; this is an underestimated strength builder.

Winners, Even They Lose Now and Then

Every athlete has setbacks. Everyone has setbacks in their lives; you don't have to be an athlete for this to happen. It is just part of life.

Champion boxers who have never been defeated are rare. But rare as they may be, there are some who go through their whole careers without losing a fight. Now, a boxer who has never lost a fight has at some time lost rounds on points. He may have been the eventual winner, but if you were to look at the judge's score cards, some of his rounds were losses. But put simply, if he wins more rounds than he loses, he wins the fight.

The great Valentino Rossi, winner of multiple MotoGP World Champion has lost some of his races. He has won far more than he's ever lost. Losing is not so bad. In fact, losing is good for athletes. The real champions gain mental strength and more determination from an occasional loss.

The real difference between champions and the rest is the champions never stop being champions. They can have a setback, have a loss, and then just get back into the job of being or becoming the champion. A real champ can lose several times in a row. But the difference is he'll examine what he's doing and change something to start the wins happening again.

The times when a loss is most difficult to take is when you don't think it's possible. When you know that an occasional loss is inevitable, you're better equipped to handle it if it comes your way.

Very often bad races and bad luck come along as a series of events. It's often described as a run of bad luck. If you're experiencing a run of bad luck, stop it right there. Don't accept a run of bad luck. It may just happen that you are faced with a couple of unfortunate incidents, one after the other.

This is a good time to get someone you trust to look at what you're doing. Quite often there are bad decisions made, one after the other, that cause the run of bad luck. How often have we heard of the athlete who had four punctures in one race? I wonder how often it was one puncture not handled properly in the first place?

Some say we make our own luck. In many cases, the luckiest people are the ones who never lose sight of how talented, how fortunate, and how grateful they are for what they have.

Motivational speakers have made fortunes by telling people to think positive. Thinking positive has to be followed by acting positive. If your positive thoughts are not backed up by your positive actions, the losses will continue.

My experience with lots of athletes shows that a great race is the next one after an athlete has a shocker. When one of my athletes makes a few bad decisions (paces badly; overfeeds himself; and turns a nine hour, thirty-minute day into a twelve hour, thirty-minute one), it never worries me. I don't get out the tissues and do a back-patting session.

I just want to know as much as I can as soon as I can about the race. We identify the problem, and then I leave the athlete to handle the situation as best as he can. Seriously, I'm not there to pat backs and wipe tears. That's your mother's job. I'm here for direction.

This approach may seem hard. But time has proven to me that the athletes who have been through the identification process with me and have been left to handle the losses are the ones who are going to make it and come back harder and meaner next time.

Winners learn from setbacks; losers dwell on them, milking all the sympathy and attention they can get.

Just when you think you can make ends meet, somebody moves the ends.

Excellence or Popularity, It's Your Choice

It really doesn't matter what field of work or sport we're involved in. We will very often have to make a choice between doing what we feel is best or doing that which will gain most popularity. It seems that teenagers face this dilemma most often.

It's been a long time since I was a teenager, but I can still remember making decisions that were really wrong at the time just so I could remain popular in my peer group. Being popular is pretty important for a teenager.

As I've grown older, I've valued doing what I feel is right, far more than being popular. I once read the saying, "I'd rather be disliked for who I am than to be liked for who I am not." As a coach, I have had pressure put on me at times to change what we do to suit an individual. It just doesn't happen.

I'm not the only one who knows the right way to do something. There are many right ways. There are many wrong ways. The results suggest that the way we're using is one of the right ways.

I've recently been amused by postings, about coaching, on a triathlon chat site. Lots of readers just read them and don't comment. About half a dozen posters, for reasons known only to themselves, will not identify themselves, and they post under invented tags. These mystery men, the keyboard captains, are making sweeping statements about how an athlete should be coached. Because they remain anonymous, it would be easy to assume that their statements are neither backed by qualifications or results.

One poster suggested a coach should not have a triathlete practice kicking or "catch-up" drills. We regularly do these drills and many more in developing our swimmers as part of a balanced plan designed to help them become more comfortable in the water and to have a better balanced position in the water. Good swimmers can kick. Triathlon swimmers don't need to kick much, but they must be able to do it efficiently to maintain good body position.

It's a simple formula: better body position = less drag = faster times.

The catch-up drill is another chance for a novice swimmer to become more balanced in the water. Most novice swimmers have trouble holding a relaxed arm out in front for a split second, without grabbing at the water. Catch-up teaches this by allowing the swimmer to become relaxed and balanced in the water. Then the actual catch (probably the most important part of a triathlete's stroke) can be trained with this drill.

Better balance + better catch = less drag + more propulsion = better times.

The same genius suggests that triathletes should not do high-cadence cycling. As a squad, over a week's work, the average cadence would probably be eighty to eighty-five revolutions per minute (this takes into account hills, strength intervals, aerobic spinning, and so on). Eighty to eighty-five revolutions per minute seems to be the most common cadence for Ironman triathletes to time trial at. We would average that over a week.

When we do "lactic-tolerance" or "VO2-max" intervals, our cadence will go as high as 110 to 120 revolutions per minute. This is how it's done, even though on race day, we'll never get to those revs. One of the missing links in the average triathlete's fitness is the well-rounded effect gained by doing some very high-cadence, high-intensity intervals. This is only 10 to 15 per cent of the athlete's work.

Large aerobic base + strength work = endurance + high VO2 max + high-lactic tolerance + high AT = faster bike splits.

One of the sad things about triathlon chat sites is the fact that unfit, inexperienced people can post training advice. Or worse, criticize those who actually work in the field and produce results in a wide range of athletes of all abilities and age groups.

There has to be a reason why a poster would use an alias.

You have the power within you to be anything you ever desired; you simply have to know what you really want.

What Missy Has Taught Me

Most mornings I wake up before 5:00 a.m. It's just a habit. I didn't have to get up that early, but with sunrise coming early, I guess my body clock is locked into the seasons. It was time to get up. I still had a little bit of office work to catch up on after a late start to the week. We had spent the week at Noosa watching a lot of friends compete in the Noosa triathlon.

To be honest, the Noosa triathlon was a reason to go away for a weekend and have a break. I had really been getting into the renovation project I was working on, and I know if I had of stayed in Brisbane, I would have worked all weekend. I love the work. If there's work in front of me, I don't feel tired. I just focus on the job but can feel smashed when I get to the end.

I have learned, over the years, that I need to schedule weekends away to give myself forced time off. It's just like a training program—three building weeks and a recovery week. Many years ago, I learned that if rest days and recovery weeks are scheduled into a program, more progress is made. Less time off training is achieved than if we rest when we feel the need to. It seems that by time we feel the need to rest, it's too late to get away with just one rest day or an easy week.

That morning after writing a couple of training programs and answering a few e-mails, I took the dogs for our usual walk to the local espresso bar. Some of the customers know them and give them a little piece of muffin or crust of raisin toast. Missy, my older dog, is in her seventeenth year. Molly is only three years old and full of energy.

Missy is half Doberman and half Australian cattle dog (blue heeler). Two years ago the vet suggested we remove her nipples, as she had lumps under them. He said they were not cancerous, but removing them would lengthen her life. In dog years, she's now well over one hundred years.

She's had a hysterectomy, she's had her breasts removed, she's not as fast as she once was, and she's a bit deaf. I think she's selectively deaf. But that's one of those things that come with age; you only have to hear what you want. But the one overriding thing about Missy is she still lives a good life. She loves her walks, she wrestles with Molly, and she still enjoys her bones and the odd can of sardines.

She has lots of friends at the coffee shop and is always ready for a fight with a stranger. The thing that impresses me about Missy is she's enjoying every day. She always has, and I reckon she will right up to the end. She's focusing on what's good in her life, not what's missing.

That morning I ran into Jimmy at the coffee shop, and while the dogs lazed around, we discussed everything from the world economy, the Afghanistan conflict, architecture, and much more. We met a few of the locals and eventually had to leave and get on with the day. As we walked home, I watched the dogs thoroughly enjoying their morning exercise. The whole experience of their lives is so simple—the smells, the encounters with others, and the company of friends. Ours can be as well. We complicate things too much.

I appreciate what I have. I am happy with my recent race in Hawaii. I couldn't do anything more on the day. It's been four weeks since the race. I am happy to be sixty-two and still able to do the Hawaii Ironman, totally healthy and uninjured right after. I'm enjoying my layoff from training; I've earned it. I have a year to get used to the idea that there are still seven men in the world in my age group who are faster than me. Or I have to do something about it.

It's up to me.

If it's to be, it's up to me.

You Live with Dog s– You Get Fleas

Last weekend I travelled to Dubbo in the middle of New South Wales to conduct a training camp/seminar. I'd been to Dubbo about thirty years ago but don't remember too much about it. It's one of those places you go through on your way to somewhere else. It is amazing where triathlon takes us. There are lots of interesting places we've travelled to that we would never have gone if it weren't for triathlon.

No, I didn't get fleas in Dubbo. I could easily get them at home. What I did get in Dubbo was inspiration. I was inspired by the camaraderie, the mateship, and the enthusiasm the "Hard Men of Dubbo" showed. They train in tough conditions in summer, which switch to hard conditions in winter. They say, "You never develop much courage if only beautiful things happen to you." I imagine a four-hour bike ride followed by a set of two-kilometre run repeats on a summer morning in Dubbo would not be described as a beautiful thing. Or a two-hour bike ride before work on a winter morning in Dubbo.

The guys feel a bit isolated and disadvantaged by living so far from major centres. It's amazing how we can feel like that, but a stranger will see our advantages. I have never spoken to a more attentive group of people. The guys out there have a real hunger for information about their sport. I do coach several of them already. This has grown from one—Simon has been with me for about a year and a half.

He reduced his Hawaii time by sixty-one minutes from one year to the next, and his Port Macquarie category place from fourteenth to fourth in one year.

This has helped recruit a few more Ironman athletes. The seminar/camp was organised by the Dubbo club, and people travelled from Orange, Bathurst, and Narromine. The monthly interclub race was to be held on a Sunday morning. This gave me the opportunity to watch the guys perform under pressure after a training day where I was able to get to know them a bit and go through lots of technique and theory. I then gave a race analysis, an areas-for-improvement report, in the afternoon lectures.

The people who are involved in triathlon in Dubbo are not disadvantaged at all. They have something special that many city athletes would be envious of.

Everywhere you go in Dubbo is ten minutes. Whether it's the airport, the bike track (a bitumen bike track around a beautiful grass playing field), or the Olympic pool. The roads are wide, and the traffic is light. There's an old saying that should be said with a drawl, "If you can't get it in Dubbo, you probably don't need it."

One of the greatest assets they have is the mateship. The great Australian mateship has it's roots in the country. In this club, they have Rob, who's the local solicitor and an organiser and leader in the group. Simon is an elite age grouper, an inspiration to the guys coming through. Two trips to Hawaii and good solid races each time. Ian is a "Hard Man." He travels all over the country, works long hours, and runs as if he still has a rugby ball under his arm. Ian's prepared to do whatever is necessary to be ready to race at Port. I told him to drop a few kilos. He's onto it; he'll be lean next time I see him.

Tim is a busy business man with a young family. He keeps the club equipment at his place and put on a great dinner for the group on Saturday night. He's a talented guy, determined to improve. Bart, the local baker, fits triathlon around a baker's lifestyle. His brother Joe, another guy with a young family and a job that requires a lot of travel, still manages to race and enjoy it. Mick is a classic Aussie larrikin, who arrived in his restored army jeep and challenged Simon for the win in the local triathlon. A hard man living a great life with his young family.

Graham; Dougal; Erica; Jody; Scott; Mark; John; Peter; and Rod, the local personal trainer, all join the other guys in mentoring young Tom. Tom is only fourteen and shows great potential. He's had a bit of time with his state junior squad but rejected their "flog the young kids to get results this year" approach. Training moderately with this great bunch of people will see him keep loving the sport and developing at a natural rate. After all, it'll be four more years before he's close to his potential.

What these lucky athletes have is hard conditions to shape them, great mates to encourage and motivate them, and strong goals to give them direction. Each one of these athletes gains something from each member of the group.

You may think the grass is greener on the other side, but if you take the time to water your own grass, it may be just as green.

The Gamblers

We could walk into any RSL or footy club in Australia at any time of the day, and there would be people on the poker machines. The clubs love it. They set the machines so they only ever pay back as much as they want. They virtually set their own profit margin. The punters playing them know they could play all day and never come out in front. But they gamble on someone else feeding the machine and then walking away just before it pays up. The long shot.

In our sport, we have gamblers as well. These are the athletes who don't eat like athletes and get away with it most of the time. But eventually poor nutrition combined with a heavy training load will take its toll. The gamblers avoid stretching because it's boring or less fun than training with their mates. They'll even skip the core-strength work because they've already got good core strength and hope it never goes away.

On race day, these gamblers are often the victims of bad luck. A good mate is a retired army officer, an engineer, an Ironman, and a wise man. He has said, "Luck is when preparation meets opportunity." Our gamblers are prepared to have a bash, hoping that what they've missed out of their program won't matter.

Everything in a training program is there for a reason. There are no fillers to make it look fat. If the plan says to do ab work three times a week, that's exactly what it means. If it says to warm up for twenty minutes before starting efforts, don't gamble with your health and fitness. Do it right.

Girls are better at following a plan than a lot of guys are. They like to tick off the boxes as they do them. Girls seem to have better attention to detail than a lot of guys do. The guys' worst mistakes are that once they start to get fit, they push too hard, too often. Some training has to be really hard, but some needs to be easy. Too hard too often is really taking a gamble with your race performances.

Like the oldies at the RSL putting their pension down the throat of the poker machines, the gamblers in our sport are usually the ones who can least afford to gamble. It's the guys with poor flexibility who are most likely to dodge a stretching session. The ones who've had a few preventable injuries already are most likely to come late and miss the group, core-strength session.

Would you drive around with no insurance? Wouldn't take the risk? Core-strength work, good nutrition, and stretching are the insurance policies for your healthy, uninjured progress through this sport.

**If you do not go after what you
want, you will never have it.**

Avoiding the Plod Can Give You Better Race Results

There's no point in practicing bad habits. When I'm on my way to the pool or out for a ride, I often see athletes out running. Two hours later I see the same athletes still running. Or should I say plodding along, dragging their tired bodies along with the most inefficient form you could imagine.

What they're doing is practicing exactly what they'll do on race day as soon as they get tired. They unconsciously tell their bodies to run that way when they're tired.

There's a much better way. Simply never run with bad form. Never run inefficiently. Learn how to run well, and practice it every time you lace up a pair of running shoes. A really useful method is to insert a short, measured walk into your long run every four or five minutes. I like to walk thirty paces every five minutes. Don't get caught up in the mathematics; it's just not important. The simple formula is to run well for a period, and then walk with good posture for a measured amount of steps.

This method often has a runner covering more ground in a ninety-minute or two-hour run than they would have if they had run continuously. The bonus is that all of the running is done technically well. The short walks are just enough to reset the mind onto the right pattern. A bit like hitting the refresh button. Some athletes fear taking up this method because they fear they'll lose the ability to run continuously. It's not a good idea to let fear be your guide. The simple fact is that you only ever run well, and that's all the body knows.

An athlete who was not happy with his result in a recent race approached me for some advice. He wondered if he should start some track sessions. The same athlete had dodged our group track sessions for the previous six weeks and had never taken advantage of the water running or leg-speed sessions the rest of the squad had been doing. Ironically, the rest of the squad were very happy with their progress in the run.

After giving this athlete the free advice, he promptly told me what he would like to do, which was quite different from what I had just advised him to do! I've seen the same athlete running along, obviously very tired, in a survival plod. Actually practicing exactly what happens in his races when he gets tired.

The same thing happens in the pool. It pays to never practice bad technique. If I am so tired that I can't hold good technique, I just get out. If I see swimmers in my squad losing it, I tell them to get out or, in some cases, put fins on to take away the fight for survival.

There's a lot of good sayings a coach accumulates along the way. One that applies here is, "Any fool can suffer."

If you do not ask, the answer will always be no.

Secret Mission Behind Enemy Lines

What are the necessary qualities to be successful in Ironman triathlon?

By successful, I mean achieving your potential. Whether that potential is winning your category, qualifying for Hawaii, or achieving a certain time. We all have our own goals, and potential is a personal thing.

I've identified some personality traits in the most successful athletes I have coached. Amazingly, they all seem to have similar traits.

Be Dependable

The athletes who can be counted on to always do their best in any conditions are the ones you would want with you on a secret mission behind enemy lines. These are the athletes who do everything on their training programs. If they can't, they check with the coach to see what is the best way to achieve the result by modifying the plan.

Be Adaptable

Face it, when you race for a whole day close to the coast, the weather conditions can change several times through the day. Things go wrong, so be ready to assess the situation and go to plan B if necessary. The ability to adapt as conditions change is a huge asset for an endurance athlete. If something does go wrong, stay cool. There's nothing to be gained by throwing your bike on the ground. Focus on what you can do, not what you can't do.

Staying Cool under Pressure

One of the greatest assets an endurance athlete can take into an event is the ability to think when thinking is necessary. My perfect Ironman athlete is a strategic thinker. There's going to be times when what you're doing is not working, and a change of strategy is necessary to be successful. Racing an Ironman is not like a fly trying to get out of a closed window. There's more to it than more trying. Too much trying and too little thinking can leave you lying on the roadside like the fly on the sill.

Be Persistent

It's rare for an Ironman athlete to be good in his first race. It's often something that has to be learned. Being told what to do is a small part of the puzzle. We're all individuals, and often we have to learn what works best for us. The best place to gain the experience is in the battle field. The guys who progress through the field are often the guys who are out there training day in, day out all year. In the rain, on windy days, and on frosty mornings, they're the ones who are always there. Persistence prevails when all else fails.

Be the Toughest SOB in Your Category

We're not born tough; we learn to be tough. If only beautiful things happen to you, you don't develop much toughness. The experiences life has thrown at you have shaped the person you are today. Seek out events and conditions that will force you to either take the soft option or the hard way. The only advantage in taking the soft option is that it's easy. If you develop the attitude of welcoming harsh conditions, you are not fazed by tough racing conditions. When the race conditions are harsh, you only have to race 10 per cent of the field, because the rest have taken their foot off the accelerator.

Be the Man I Would Choose

If I were going on a mission behind enemy lines, a mission where danger and difficulty were inevitable, I would choose certain people for my team. Some I would leave out. If you wonder if you would be chosen, you probably wouldn't be. If you know that you have the qualities listed above, you're a likely candidate to be chosen. The person who has all the qualities listed above is going to be successful in this sport.

It's what you learn after you know it all that counts.

Living in the Moment—Racing without Thinking

It doesn't matter how much I read or how much I experience training athletes to endurance events; I keep coming back to the fact that endurance events are more mental than physical. I've read about Tibetan monks who can run huge distances across mountain trails on almost no food, with times that would make them very competitive in ultra-distance running events around the world.

It seems their secret is the meditative mental state they're able to get into, where they simply allow their bodies to run without interference from their minds. It seems that driving ourselves hard is not as productive as allowing our bodies to perform without interference.

I see that interference every day when coaching swimmers. Analysis paralysis is alive and well in the triathlon community. People try too hard to get good at what they're trying to master. They're actually interfering in the natural movement of their bodies by trying too hard to control what's happening.

I often use the analogy of a dog chasing a ball. The dog only sees the ball; its sole objective is to get the ball. The dog doesn't think about foot placement, aerodynamics, and so on. All he sees is the ball and is focused on getting it. Even if you throw the ball across the highway, the dog will not see the oncoming cars; he'll only see the ball.

As endurance athletes, if we were able to tune out of controlling and hold focus on our end goals like the dog, we could move more freely. We could avoid some of the injuries people suffer that are caused by unnatural control of movements.

We need to spend a little time each workout on letting it happen. Be able to switch from making it happen to letting it happen. The Ironman race is 70 per cent mental. Yet we spend most of our training hours swimming, cycling, and running, with almost no time devoted to the mental side of the sport.

Most of us don't have lots of spare time to spend meditating. Many of us have difficulty in shutting down the thoughts racing through our minds.

I suggest spending a little part of each workout just living in the moment. Counting strokes when swimming, counting revs when cycling up a hill, or counting steps when we run can have the effect of bringing our minds back into the present moment, rather than thinking ahead of ourselves or going over the past. Meditation does not have to mean sitting cross-legged in front of a candle.

Meditation for the Ironman can be done at race pace. It's simply living in the moment and monitoring simple feedback like how the ground feels underfoot. Or feeling the breeze on your face and being aware of the environment around you, being part of that environment. Better results will come when you stop thinking about outcomes and start living the moment.

The skill to shut out the pain or discomfort of racing will not come easy. It has to be practiced. We have many hours of training ahead of us where we could practice these skills. We get to know how good technique feels. We need to gradually take ownership of those feelings so that when we clear our minds of thoughts, our bodies can keep producing perfect technique.

If you do not step forward, you will always be in the same place.

Doing What You Love—It's Easy

I know lots of people who struggle to fit everything into their busy lives. We all have work, family, and social responsibilities. In fact, fitting things in becomes another source of stress. If finding time to fit in what you love doing is causing stress, it might be time to step back and sort out what your priorities are.

If we set the alarm really early to go on holidays, it's no trouble to get up. If we set it at the same time to get up early to catch up on some work for a deadline, it's a real drag to get out of bed. The only difference is the reason we're getting up. I find if I'm meeting someone for a training session, it's much easier to get out of bed in the dark. Especially if I enjoy the other person's company.

To make progress in this sport of ours, we must be consistent with our training. That's week in, week out; month after month; and year after year. If you don't enjoy training, you really need to find another sport. This sport is 95 per cent training and 5 per cent racing.

Changing the way we look at certain workouts and learning to love them can make the job of getting there and starting so much easier. I personally love my training sessions. I love the early mornings. I love the social interaction with the guys and girls at training. We have good humour in every session, no matter how hard the session is.

My own strategy in life is to do what I love first. Do what I like next. Then do what I have to do third. I still get everything done, but I start each day with a reward. I pay myself first. I've found that starting each day with what I love to do sets up my whole day to be more productive. It sets the mood for the day.

My own days always start with my nutritional routine. I start the day with the juice of a lemon in a little bit of water. This starts my digestive system going. It sort of "wakes up my stomach." Then I prepare my pre-workout drink, even if I'm not training. I take my vitamin supplements and oil supplements with this drink. This routine is important to me. It's the first step in rewarding myself. Some people pamper themselves with chocolates, cookies, and pastries. I pamper myself with good nutrition. I value my health and choose to look after myself.

I suggest people who have the freedom to organise their own schedules should try the approach of "love" first, "like" second, and "have to" third. Learn to love your training, and you'll make more progress. The people I have met in this sport are overachievers. They always get done what they have to do. But in some cases, they put these important things in front of their own happiness.

If you deny yourself the opportunity to be happy, before you know it, your productivity starts to drop off, and sadness gradually replaces happiness. Start each day with what you love. Love yourself first. Then you'll be in a better frame of mind to give more of yourself to others.

Life is like a camera. Focus on what you want, capture the good times, and develop from the negatives. And if things don't work out, take another shot.

No Spark When You Need It in Your Race

I can't count the number of guys who, over the years, have not raced an Ironman at the speed their training suggested they should. There's all sorts of reasons for their unsatisfying performances.

Some have simply built the day up into something to be feared. It's not to be feared. It must be respected, but there's nothing to fear. I once stood beside a young athlete waiting to go down to the swim start, maybe twenty minutes before race start, and his heart-rate monitor was showing 126 beats per minute. I looked at mine, and it was fifty-five beats per minute. This was his first Ironman race, but he was seriously worried about what he was about to face. He didn't race to his potential. In fact, he was about ninety minutes slower than I expected.

I've seen others affect their outcomes by overanalysing every part of the race to the point of becoming a slave to the figures. I've found that focusing on the figures too closely in racing can actually make achieving the right figures extremely difficult. We're all different. Some of us work in very conservative jobs, where absolutely no risks are ever taken. Watching the figures too closely can cause the athlete to become too mechanical and lose the freedom of movement from which great performances come.

Another common method that can cause a disappointing result is thinking of what others are doing. Focusing outside of your own square metre cannot help what's going on inside your square metre. There's only one person's result you can influence on race day. Focus on yourself.

In fact, too much thinking will undermine your performance. You're not there to think; you're there to swim as efficiently as possible. Ride as efficiently as you can, and get off and run as efficiently as possible. The best results come from applying 90 per cent effort all day long, always being able to go harder if you wanted to but choosing not to. The plan for 90 per cent effort often turns out the best outcome.

Another method athletes employ in their training that produces unsatisfying results is the constant testing method. In every session, the athlete is focused on the outcome. Every session has to reach certain targets, speeds, power figures, and so on. Often these athletes have spent too much emotional energy driving themselves to reach these targets. And on race day, they lack the reserves of mental energy to drive themselves over the last couple of hours when it really counts.

So many athletes overlook the need to be mentally fresh for an Ironman race. One of the strategies likely to get you to the start line without the mental freshness necessary to perform is starting the buildup too early. Experience has shown that the ideal buildup time for an Ironman race is twelve to sixteen weeks. It's okay to train for a year with the Ironman as the long-term goal. But you need to be investing your mental energy into intermediate goals so that when you reach sixteen weeks out, you turn on your focus to the main game.

It's more important to be mentally prepared and a little underdone physically than the opposite scenario. There are too many slaves to their training diaries. No one has ever asked to see your training diary when you step up onto the podium. In the month before a major race, it's important to have your relationships running smoothly. If your partner is making you feel guilty for training, you're unlikely to do the job well on race day. The last month is a crucial time to get your house in order. Promise whatever you have to. Skip a training session to support your supporters. It'll pay off to have a happy home and a happy workplace. When the pressure is on, you'll have no background noise.

Tinley once said, "Endurance is a state of mind." Arrive at the start line with a healthy, uninjured body; a strong purpose; and a fresh mind, and you'll race to your potential.

Live a life shaped by optimism; it's a far better option than a life shaped by fear.

When You Think It's All You Have, You Have 20 Per Cent More

Average members of the public never find their physical limits. In fact, most never go anywhere near their limits.

Most have no interest in getting out of their comfort zones. In fact, most will not ever really experience any more than discomfort. Most conversations around the average work lunch room are complaints about how cold it is, how hot it is, how far someone had to walk, or how bad the weather has been.

Most have no desire to do what we do for "fun." In fact, they cannot imagine why anyone would want to explore the limits of endurance and pain tolerance. But for those addicted to the exploration of human limits, it's just what we do. I'm sure many of us don't really stop to think why we do these long and often painful events.

In a society where kids are raised as though they're wrapped in cotton wool, where they're discouraged from any sort of risk-taking games, and where they never go barefoot, there's a natural urge to compete. It's a tragedy to take competition out of school games. It doesn't prepare the kids for the real world, where they're going to have to compete and often endure being beaten by others who want the prize more than they do.

In most cases, being beaten by the person who is prepared to suffer more discomfort or pain depends on which angle you look at it from. The ability to fight for what you want and to put yourself through real pain to get it can be learned. Every day the athlete wakes up, he or she is faced with the opportunity to add to this talent. It is a talent built layer by layer. Every day the athlete beats the hold of the warm bed and throws the covers off to go out and work on dreams takes him or her one step closer.

Getting out of a warm bed and going to train with your mates is not pain; it's barely discomfort. In fact, it's an act of reaffirming your goals. Every time trial, every hill repeat, and every over distance session is testing the limits of the individual. Little tests often have a way of teaching you where "the edge" is. But don't be fooled; this is not the edge. This is where your safety valve lets you get to before saying, "This is enough; any more and I could hurt myself."

This pain barrier is there to save you. Elite athletes know it's a false edge; it's not the edge at all. The real edge is 20 per cent farther away. It's not practical to go to the edge in every session, but it is very valuable knowledge to know that where you go in training is only to prepare you to go farther on race day. That's why developing athletes gain a lot from regular racing. They get to explore the boundaries of their own physiology.

Many of us bump up against the barrier and think that's as far as we can go. This barrier is there to keep the mediocre, mediocre. The winners go up to that barrier and don't knock on the door; they kick the door down and go straight inside. If you have big goals, take my word on it. Those goals lie on the other side of your invisible barrier. To unlock the door to that area, you have to be fit. You have to be fresh, both physically and mentally.

If you're not mentally fresh, you'll have difficulty in driving yourself to the limits. A lot of self-coached Ironman athletes are overtrained, not only physically but also mentally. A taper is as important for mental freshness as it is for physical freshness. If you want to cross that barrier into the winner's zone, taper well, and leave out those last-minute cramming workouts. They'll probably cost you much more than you'll gain.

Make sure your own direction is clear. Most free advice is tainted by the advisors own fears.

It's a Blueprint, Not a Menu

When their training program arrives in their inbox, most athletes quickly scan through it to see what's in store for the next month. I'm often told it's an exciting time, looking forward to the next four-week block.

Our recent Hawaii qualifiers from the Cairns Ironman had one thing in common; they treated the training program like a blueprint. The way a construction supervisor treats the plans—no deviation from the plan. They treated everything on the program as important.

A lot of athletes have told me their goals. In fact, we have to establish well-defined goals before we start working together. I ask for long-term goals, five-year goals, and intermediate goals for along the way. One-year, three-month, and even smaller steps make up the missing pieces of the puzzle.

It's really important to have a plan in place and to steadily tick off the boxes, one by one. This process is not new. It's incredibly important in building confidence and self-belief in the athlete. The simple process of doing all the little steps along the way unleashes something inside the athlete's mind, especially when the end goals are very clear. The more often the goals are sighted, the more ownership the athlete takes over them.

I know a lot of athletes who want something, but they just don't want it bad enough to look after the details. They read their training programs more like a restaurant menu, with a list of workouts from which to choose—ones they'd like to do and ones they'd like to leave out. I see it all the time. Some are reading blueprints, and some are reading menus.

Many of us do the sport for fun and don't have strong goals. There's nothing wrong with this approach. After all, most of us are not in it for the prize money. I'm aiming at the people who are out to achieve bigger goals, who have specific things they would like to achieve in this sport. They have a definite time frame in which they would like to achieve them.

The blueprint people find it easier to drive themselves when the going gets really tough, and in Ironman racing, it is going to get really tough at some stage. The ones who pick and choose from the menu simply have not invested enough in the process to really take ownership of the goal and, as a consequence, find it easier to find excuses (reasons to quit).

The blueprint people have bought and paid for their prize a long time ago. When they race, they're not trying to get their hands on something. They already have it. And when they race, they defend it. They dare someone else to come up and try to take it away. It's been paid for in every early morning, in every core-strength session, and in every run off the bike they were supposed to do. If the plan says run twelve times one-kilometre repeats off the bike, they don't stop at eight.

Every ten-minute core session and every set of run drills that seem to be doing nothing are adding to better run technique and a better posture. So often it's these simple little things that can give the blueprint people a five-minute advantage. Knowing you did everything possible and wanting the prize so badly you're prepared to put your body through hell will add up to closer to a thirty-minute advantage.

Every day, every sunrise is an opportunity to do something toward your goals. Make sure that you have done something toward those goals before the sun sets.

The Optional Extras—Often the Difference

Often when I write training programs, I include some optional extra swims, core work, or runs. I purposely put these in as optional as a test. I rarely find out if they've been done. But the athletes know if they've done them. Every time they look at their programs and either take the easy option or do the optional sessions, they're either reinforcing their determination to do well or missing opportunities to build a rock-solid mental base.

Most of the time, those optional, extra sessions are of very small physical benefit, but they are of more benefit than doing nothing. You'll hear people excuse them away as junk miles, or they'll come up with lots of good reasons and excuses why they didn't get around to doing them. The excuses are the nails that hold the house of failure together.

The execution of a race is at least 70 per cent mental. Most of your competitors will arrive in similar physical condition to you. Observe the people around you at work or socially, and listen to the excuses they make for everything they don't feel like doing. The athletes we compete with are drawn from a similar section of society; only they've discovered a sport that stands them above their lazier friends. Even though our athlete friends are much more motivated, their conversations are full of excuses.

If any of us go into an event with a reason for a less than perfect performance, we've already shot ourselves in the foot. We all have hiccups in our preparations, but every day is an opportunity to do the little things and build rock-solid confidence in our abilities. Sometimes the optional extra session is a short run with some drills included. Run drills are the sort of thing that so many feel are unproductive, but the leaders of every category in an Ironman have better technique from many around them and far better than the back of the field. Technique matters, especially when you're tired.

You owe it to your parents to give whatever you try your best shot. Feel their belief in you as a tailwind on your back. No one wants you to achieve more than they do.

It Takes Courage to Sign Up for Your First Ironman; Fear Is a Good Thing

It's not the same sort of courage that it takes to face an enemy who's trying to kill you. But it still takes something special to sign up for an event that will challenge you to your known limits and beyond. The event you have signed up for has the chance of breaking you both physically and mentally. Part of you wants to test yourself, while another part of you fears the test. But you have signed up anyway.

The word *courage* means different things to different people. Being courageous is a habit. It can be a way of living. A state of mind where you just do what you have to do, regardless of what that little voice in your head says to talk you out of it. We all have that little voice, but it can be reasoned with. People who live courageously listen to the little voice in their heads, but the commitment to the task is strong enough to put the protests of the negative little voice aside.

So to live courageously, you first need to be committed to the task. Along the way to that first Ironman race, your commitment is going to be tested many times. The training program is going to put obstacles in your way that will test your level of commitment and give you the courage to do the right thing.

I have a book in my collection simply called *Courage*. It's written by Osho, an Indian spiritual teacher. He describes courage as "not the absence of fear, but the total presence of fear, with the courage to face it." My experience is that your strength lies directly behind your fear. By standing up to your fears and busting through them, you discover your full strength on the other side.

Basically courage is about facing fear. Accept that fear is normal. Everyone has fears. By accepting it as a normal emotion and not something that you, alone, have to face will make your journey much less lonely. Knowing that you're not the only one going through this emotion makes it all feel a lot more okay.

I asked my good friend Lt. Col. Ret. George Hulse, a man for whom I have the greatest admiration and respect, what his definition of courage was. George has been a career soldier and a natural leader, who has faced and survived situations that most of us will fortunately never have to face. He's a special human and a total gentleman. A friend described him as the Hugh Jackman of triathlon. (All the guys would like to be like him, and all the girls love him.)

George said, "It takes courage to go into a place you'd rather avoid, but you trust yourself to know you'll come out the other end okay."

George's definition points out the need to trust yourself. This is one of the critical qualities we'll be working on in our training, building that trust in ourselves. We'll go through enough challenging experiences in our buildup to develop that trust. When you trust another person, you know that you can depend on that person in a difficult situation. It's no different when you learn to trust yourself.

Over the next few months, we'll be working together to build that trust.

Quality simply means care for detail; you owe it to yourself to only deliver excellence.

Keep a Diary, and Build Trust in Yourself

It takes courage to do things that scare you. But doing those things requires you to trust yourself. Trust yourself that you'll make the right decisions at the right time. A lot of pre-race nerves are based on the fear that we'll not do what we normally do in training. Like many fears, it's totally based on self-doubt.

Most of us have more ability than we believe. In fact, it's often the coach's job to drag out that performance by kicking down the barriers we have set up around us. Just because you have never done it before, doesn't mean you can't do it now.

Most of our supporters actually have more faith in us than we often do. A little exercise I encourage nervous athletes to do is write a list of their fears. All the things that are worrying them about their impending races. Then they make a list of all of their supporters—family, friends, training buddies. Now as they go through the list of supporters, they have a thought about what it is that makes those people believe in them.

In most cases, people believe in you because you have a history of doing the right thing. You're dependable. Supporters are used to seeing you achieve whatever you have set out to do. They trust you to make the right decision at the right time. They trust you to be the best you can be, because that's what you do in all other parts of your life.

This sport attracts overachievers. The people I am fortunate to coach are all at the top of their games; whatever that occupation is, they're leaders. These people are dependable by nature. They're honest. When they look in the mirror at the end of the day, they know they have given their best.

If you happen to be a little worried about the race you've committed yourself to, take a look in your rear-view mirror at the rest of your life. If people trust you to always do your best and if you've done everything on your program, trust the program. Trust yourself.

The price of being a sheep is boredom; the price of being a wolf is loneliness. Choose carefully.

Resilience

Most of us are in the game for health benefits, enjoying the company of other people with similar interests, and keeping our minds and bodies tuned together. Let's face it; training is where all the benefits come from. Maintaining the best health possible allows us to train very regularly, giving us the consistency that gives us the best improvement.

Often when people become athletes, their first year or two are the most challenging to stay healthy. Lots of people don't realise that optimum health is not just the absence of illness. There are a lot of people out there who are not actually sick but are far from optimum health.

The resilience that seasoned endurance athletes often enjoy is the ability to train all year without illness or injury. This ability to tolerate exposure to the public and not catch every cold that goes through their offices and to run for three hours without becoming injured is what I call resilience.

This resilience comes from achieving a balance in life, a balance in which we recognize that we can't do everything. We often cannot do the volume of training that some others can. And we often don't need to. It comes from eliminating excesses from our lives—too much stress and too much high-intensity training. It comes from too few vegetables in the diet and not enough sleep.

On my new-athlete, training-program questionnaire is the request for a three-day food diary. In almost 80 per cent of cases, this is the first area of an athlete's life that needs adjusting. Then I look through the athlete's previous training records. So often I find a common pattern of, "Train for four to five weeks, get sick, lose two weeks, and start again."

We adjust the training load to something below what was making the athlete vulnerable to every minor illness that came through the air-conditioning system. Then we balance the diet so the body is getting the right fuel for performance and recovery. To this we add the right nutritional supplements to cover any shortfalls in the athlete's diet. Then we start to develop the resilience we seek. Often a new athlete's immune system is underperforming. The right dietary supplements can boost this, but it's often not a quick fix. In a lot of cases, it took years to run the immune system down; it can't be rebuilt in a couple of weeks.

Once I look at the athlete's short-term and long-term goals, my intentthen becomes to get that athlete to those goals without illness or injury. An important part of that process, once the volume and diet have been balanced, is to work on developing the very best technique in each sport.

Physiotherapists agree that if athletes have good technique, good flexibility, good nutrition, and good core strength and are not overtrained, they will not suffer injuries. As long they can avoid accidents.

The resilience I seek is born from balance.

If you train hard, you'll not only be hard but also hard to beat.

Training the Top Three Inches

Lots of athletes are winners in training but, unfortunately, are FORDs: F***ed on race day. We all laugh about it amongst our mates, but it's so disappointing after all the hard work to not get the results they deserve.

Any successful Ironman athlete will readily tell you it's all in the head. Yet in most cases, 95 per cent of the athlete's training time is spent on training everything except the top three inches. One of the hardest jobs a coach can face is when an athlete has failed to deliver on race day, and he looks to the coach for the answer. Not many are ready to accept personal responsibility.

I've seen athletes blame the guy who mixed the drinks at the aid stations, the weather, their equipment, and even their families for disrupting their sleep patterns. It usually has to be handled delicately, as egos are fragile. The sooner athletes accept the facts, the sooner they can start the process of building an optimum mental state to get the best out of their bodies.

Desire is one of the most powerful tools in building the mental state we seek. You have to know just what you want and what you're prepared to do to get it. Often the goals are too vague; often they're not held with enough passion. Wanting something is not the same as being truly hungry for it.

Being prepared to do whatever it takes is another area where athletes often let themselves down. Wanting something is quite different from being committed to getting it. I've heard it said, "Success is easy; you just have to decide what you're prepared to give up to get it."

Adaptability is pure mental toughness. It seems too simple. The toughest athletes are adaptable. They'll be ready to adapt to suit the conditions in seconds. They'll go from "poor me" to "go harder" in a split second. The softest athletes I've ever met were softened by their mothers (my own theory). When I was growing up, if we got a bit of gravel rash in a fall, my dad poured kerosene over it. Cheap, readily available antiseptic. If we stood on a nail, kerosene. The first aid kit in a can. If the wound was bad enough, my mum would tear some strips of old bed sheet off and bandage it with that.

Honestly, I had never had a Band-Aid on my body until I was in my twenties. I have a friend who thinks we may be related. He was raised on a cattle property out west and had the same first-aid kit. He is a dependable, tough mate who someone could count on in any situation.

I have met guys who would have had a Band-Aid on for just about their whole childhood. Every mosquito bite, every scratch. Is it any wonder that they grow up to be sooks? If Mummy fusses over every knock and bump, our little boy grows up and seeks out a mummy substitute to look after him. It's not going to be me. Coaches are for direction; mothers are for sympathy.

Harden up. Get used to things not going right. Adapt to them. Whingeing is for losers. Winners don't need excuses; they don't whinge. If you feel yourself about to complain about something, pause a moment, and ask yourself, could I adapt to this?

When we race the Australian Ironman, things are not going to go like clockwork for everybody. Some things will go wrong for some people. Are we ready for that? Are we just going to pour kerosene on it and get back into it, or are we going to go looking for a Band-Aid?

How bad do you want that result? Do you even know what it is you really want? Can you see yourself actually getting it? Are you game to speak out exactly what it is that you're aiming for?

Tell your mates what you're going for. Harden up, and do what it takes to get it. It's all in the top three inches.

When you look at your times and see no change but still have faith, know that if you stick at it, you will get there. That's the difference between those who succeed and those who fail.

Consistency Gets Results

Consistency is no doubt the most important part of an Ironman training program. It often involves a lot of rather boring work that simply has to be done.

One of the greatest challenges for an Ironman coach is to present a program that delivers consistency over a long term without becoming boring. It's mentally very difficult to hold a goal for a whole year or for several years. The long-term goal has to be split up into several intermediate goals so the athlete can see the goal posts within striking distance. Our time-trial series can be good for this purpose.

Training through winter can deliver the athlete to the start of the next season at a higher level than at the end of the previous season. But this strategy has pitfalls. I've found athletes cannot do the same number of training hours in winter that they could in the warmer months. It seems humans have a hibernation program built into them that switches on during winter when the days are shorter.

We've all seen how flower farms manipulate the length of day with lights or blackout curtains to fool the plants into flowering out of season. By shortening the length of day for a couple of weeks and then lengthening the day by opening the curtains earlier each day, spring flowering plants will burst into life and produce. That's why poinsettias are available as Christmas flowers in the northern winter, when they naturally flower in spring, as they do in Australia. They've been fooled. The nurserymen make a fortune from them by supplying colour in drab old cities like Chicago, Boston, and New York.

Us highly sophisticated modern humans in our climate-controlled homes and cars are still affected by the length of day. Just watch how much easier it is to train when spring starts to show in longer days. You are an animal, and you have remained relatively unchanged for fifty thousand years. The seasons do affect you.

Because winter does affect us, we have to train carefully at this time of year. We have to reduce training hours to stay healthy. We're all different and have different tolerances to workload. It's our job to work closely with our coaches to find just what we can handle to stay well.

Noticing the signs of overtraining is a valuable skill to develop. A little tickle in the back of the throat can be the first sign. Increasing the vitamin C dose to double the present rate can fix this immediately. Taking colloidal silver per the manufacturers' directions can also be very helpful (available from health-food stores).

But the one thing most of us need more of in winter is sleep. Man is designed to sleep more in winter. Crops are harvested in fall; winter is a time of rest and maintenance. Spring is the time for planting and harder work.

So, if we go with the flow of energy, we'll do the sort of training that will set us up for greater gains in spring. We'll work on technique. We'll keep the work low intensity for most of the workload. We'll work on improving core strength and flexibility. We'll sleep in when we need to so we don't slip over the edge and become sick, losing a week or two that might have been saved by having a day off.

After the winter solstice or shortest day of the year in the southern hemisphere, we'll be able to do slightly more training as our bodies react to nature's clock. Until it's really noticeable and the mornings are sunny again, we have to be careful to do what we can.

Doing a little bit often and over a long time is more productive then doing a lot for a short time and then losing a few weeks through illness. Go with the flow.

Sometimes the best you can do is not analyse, not obsess, and not lose faith. Just relax, do the basics right, and hold the belief that things will work out.

Thoroughbreds and Work Horses

When we know a couple of hundred athletes, we can easily identify some as thoroughbreds and some as workhorses. The thoroughbreds are able to advance quickly. They seem to gain more from their training. Let's face it; they have a natural gift.

Then we notice that some others have a fantastic work ethic. They may have a little less talent than the thoroughbreds do, but through sheer dedication and persistence, they're able to achieve great things in this sport. It seems that in Ironman racing, an athlete with a little less natural talent but a great work ethic can achieve very exciting results. Quite often the naturally gifted athletes (the thoroughbreds) are lazy trainers. I've seen them train well for a short time, make great gains, and then lose interest. While the workhorse may have been left behind initially, when the talented thoroughbred strays off the training path, the workhorse gradually works his way past.

A squad can benefit from having both types of athlete. The thoroughbreds can set a pace and standard for the workhorse to aspire to. The workhorses can be a huge asset to the thoroughbreds. They can provide the training structure, the dependability, and the company that makes a squad great. The example of tenacity and perseverance set by the workhorses does not go unnoticed by the thoroughbreds. Each athlete type provides something for the other.

Workhorses train well together, pushing each other and the thoroughbreds to greater heights. A squad made up of a small handful of thoroughbreds is rarely as successful as a squad made up of mostly good, reliable workhorses. A culture of hard work and attention to detail will produce more podium performances than a small group of specialists.

We need both types of athlete to get the best out of the squad as a whole. Know where you fit. If you were not a sports star all the way through school, there's a good chance you'll have to achieve through consistent hard work. Even if you were a sports star at school, if you don't do the consistent work, a workhorse is going to kick your butt in your next race.

You can't calm the storm. What you can do is calm yourself, and then the storm will pass.

Details, How Important Are They?

I have often said I'm not a details person; I'm a big picture man.

That's not entirely correct. I hope I haven't misled too many. I really don't care whether you have a carbon, an aluminium, or a titanium bike. As long as you're set up pretty right and you ride it hard. I don't care if your shoes are twenty grams less than another brand is. As long as you don't walk in the marathon, I'm happy.

For me the details that do make the difference are the ones I insist on throughout the year.

* Doing your ab work correctly (sucking in your stomach when you do leg extensions). If you have not done your core-strength work correctly, you may as well ride a postman's bike.

* Stretching. My eighty-year-old mother is more flexible than some of the athletes in my squad. Yet they consider the aerodynamic advantages of mounting water bottles behind themselves rather than on the frame to lessen the drag as they power through the bike leg. It won't matter where they mount their bottles if they have to sit up half the bike because they're too inflexible to touch their toes. There's not much advantage in having

a time-trial bike if your bike-fit guy packs your head stem up another inch.

* I've recently seen bike-fit guys changing crank lengths on athletes' bikes by 2.5 millimetres. If you're flexible, you wouldn't even notice the change. I have ridden crank lengths from 170 to 180 over a period of eighteen months with no adverse or beneficial effects. How much do these guys charge? I'm not saying proper bike fit is not important, but the changes should not be made to justify the cost of the service.

* When I tell someone to eat protein at every meal, I don't mean a little bit of skim milk on corn flakes. When I tell people to take Opti after each workout, I mean a real serving of it. Then follow it up with a real meal. Next time you race, we're going to check your time, not your skinfolds!

* When I tell you that fats are very important in your diet, the two flaxseed oil capsules a.m. and p.m. are not your total fat intake for the day. If you're shivering in pool water that's twenty-four or twenty-five degrees, something is wrong. The omega-3 oils found in cold-water fish are the "antifreeze" that allows fish to swim under arctic ice with no problems. They are also the raw materials from which your body makes many of your important hormones. Another reason why some people feel the cold more than others is low blood sugar. Have

a piece of toast with peanut butter before swimming, and see if that makes a difference. Peanut butter also contains fat. This is good; fats are your friends.

*   When you're swimming, breathing bilaterally is really important. It balances your body; you pull evenly with each arm. You swim a straight line in open water. And on race day, you have options. Head position dictates leg position. Good head position means less drag and faster swimming.

*   Getting there on time. To some it's a minor detail. They'll always have an excuse or a reason for being late. If they can find an excuse for being late for training, they'll find an excuse for not racing to their potential on race day. It's just as easy to get there on time as it is to continuously get there ten minutes late. If I, as the coach, always arrived five to ten minutes late, would the message be that I no longer care?

So, some details are very important. But I don't really need to know what your core temperature is at the moment. I don't want to know the colour of your urine or the consistency of your stools.

Train smart, and race hard. When in doubt, go harder.

Never give up on a dream because of the time it will take. The time will pass anyway.

Colloidal Silver

Often, as an athlete gets close to an event, his or her immune system struggles to keep on top of the bugs that try to get hold of him or her in the last few weeks.

In a perfect world, athletes get to take a nap each day, take nutritional supplements, and have a fabulous diet with lots of fresh fruit and veges. Their training is structured to stress them just enough to bring about the improvements they're seeking. Unfortunately, most of us have jobs and families that add to our workload. We often get pushed right to the edge.

When we feel the first signs of illness—the slightly sore throat, the slight headache, legs that just don't want to ride up hills, and arms that have trouble pulling back the blankets to let us up in the morning—that's the time to have a rest day. Having an unscheduled rest day at the right time may save two-week's training and the subsequent loss of confidence that often comes from sitting around while your mates are out training.

These are the steps I take when I find myself in that position:

* I rest immediately.

* I double or sometimes even triple my vitamin C intake (1000 milligrams every three hours).

* I sprinkle the contents of a zinc capsule on my tongue and, with a little water, gargle it (zinc lozenges do the same job).

* I take one dessert spoonful of colloidal silver and gargled in a little water before swallowing. (Colloidal silver is a tasteless, clear liquid available from just about any health-food store.) It was used in hospitals long before antibiotics were invented. I take it every four hours for a day or two.

This simple procedure along with rest and warm, well-cooked foods, soups, and stews are enough to bounce me back to good health in a day or so. I'm attacking the bugs rather than letting them get a hold on me.

I keep these supplements in the cupboard ready for emergencies. They may not stop every attack on our immune systems, but they have saved a lot of us from losing two-week's training when we really come down with something.

If symptoms persist, consult your health-care professional. (That's what they say; isn't it?)

Pain is inevitable; suffering is optional.

Ongoing Development of the Athlete

Often I'm asked why are we doing mountains if the next race we're going to do is flat? Why are we doing backstroke when all we need to be able to do is freestyle? Why do we do hypoxic breathing workouts so often? Why run at a pace slower than race pace so often?

The answer to all of the above is that I'm training my athletes to develop them to their potential. I'm not training them to one race down the road.

That's not going to happen in three months. It's widely accepted in coaching circles that it takes seven years to fully develop an aerobic system. It's extremely rare for anyone to ever get to the Olympics in either swimming, cycling, or running in fewer than ten years. That's not ten years of watching the Tour de France on television. That's ten years of early mornings and cold fingers and toes.

The group of athletes I have just trained to the Australian Ironman are only part of the way down their development trails. Some are several years down the trail, and some are only two years into the journey.

Most likely some of my group have as much talent as Vernay (the winner) or Anderson (second place). The only way this talent can be released is by doing the "hard yards." That's buildup after buildup, not continuous slogging.

The only way we can keep the passion going is to commit to an event not too distant into the future. About sixteen weeks is an ideal time. That sixteen-week period can then be broken down into a base-building period and a sharpening, race-specific period.

Once the event is reached, the performance is evaluated and the lessons learned. Then it's time for recovery. The length of recovery depends on the length and intensity of the race.

Usually after an Ironman, I give the guys two weeks off training to sleep in, go to the movies, and have a bit of normal life. During that time, we keep all of the dietary supplements up. This is a critical time to support the immune system.

After the recovery break, we go into another build phase. It's good to find another goal race twelve to sixteen weeks away. If the next important event is twenty-four to twenty-six weeks away, it's too far to maintain focus, and another training goal can be placed about eight weeks away. A time trial or a smaller, less important event can become the object to focus on.

It's always important to have a destination to aim at. Training without a goal can become meaningless, and it's just too hard to get out of bed.

The overriding principle is that in order to reach your potential, you have to be "at it" year in, year out.

It's good to have a race every year to test the progress in your development. I have used the Gold Coast marathon over several years as a test race. The overall result is not important to me, as I'm simply using the race to develop as an Ironman triathlete.

Running the marathon three years in a row at set heart rates has given me a real measurable performance to test my progress. The same can be done with bike time trials. Especially mountain time trials. These types of tests are far cheaper than lab tests are and just as accurate.

It is very important to keep records. Times, dates, and so on. It's good to see how the plan is unfolding.

Everyone wants to eat but few want to hunt.

Be Specific with Your Goals for the Season

In the southern hemisphere, when we're about to start laying the foundations for our season, we use that time to choose goals. And we plan to achieve them.

When a new athlete comes to me, I always ask what we're working toward achieving. It's surprising how often they really don't know exactly what they're aiming at. They have a few ideas of what they'd like. It's more of a wish list than a set of goals.

Goals for the season don't have to be times. They don't have to be positions in categories.

The goals for the season could be like the following:

* To go faster than ever before. We then need to identify what speed we have swum, cycled, or run in the past and to set mini-goals throughout the season or time trials in each sport to gradually inch our way down to the "faster than ever before" time. By breaking the distances down into smaller pieces, we can get used to actually swimming, cycling, or running at the faster speeds. Every time we perform at that faster speed, we gain confidence. Lots of small confidence-building steps along the way build a wall of confidence. The longer races are built on confidence.

* To be leaner and lighter than ever before. Dropping a couple of kilos can raise our VO2 max significantly. There's no point starving ourselves and looking like a refugee if it leaves us with no energy to train. The easy way to achieve this goal is to eat for performance. To train well, we need fuel; to recover well, we need protein and carbs at the right time. The best plan is to not get too fat in the off season. A little restraint can let us live good lives, enjoying lots of little treats as long as we don't over indulge.

I have found little things like cutting out desserts and drinking black coffee instead of milk-based coffees. Cutting out deep fried foods and pastries. Increasing rice and vegetable intake. By following these few simple tips and training well, our goals will be easily achieved.

* The goals can be more advanced. Like gaining a Hawaii spot, winning an age group, or winning overall. These goals are for the more advanced athletes who "have the runs on the board" already. There's greater pressure involved when we get this specific.

But believe me; it ain't gonna happen if it's not a serious goal. Have dreams. We all have dreams, but when we really want something, we have to know exactly what we want and then make a solid plan of how to get it.

Once that plan is in place, every right decision we make like not having that second drink or not going out on that late night is justifiable. Discipline delivers results. Discipline only happens when an athlete has a plan.

Sometimes the smallest step in the right direction ends up being the biggest step in your life. Go carefully if you must, but take the step.

Athletes and Bulldozers, What Do They Have in Common?

When you've been around nearly sixty years, you've had a lot of time to do a lot of different things. Hopefully you've learned from each of those experiences.

In my early twenties I practiced karate for a few years. It's amazing how close to triathlon training martial arts training really is. Thousands of repetitions of each movement done perfectly until all the body knows is perfect technique. The end result is that under pressure, you don't have to think what to do or how to do it. You just do it. A bit like the Nike add.

One of the businesses I established and continued for around ten years involved buying new Cat machinery and operating an earthmoving/landscaping business. The reliability and longevity of earthmoving machinery is heavily dependent on maintenance.

Caterpillar machinery is the undisputed king of machinery. The company supports owners like no other company in the world. One of the services they offer owners is called SOS—scheduled oil sampling. By taking samples of engine, transmission, and final-drive oils at regular intervals, these samples are analysed in the lab to detect wear and help schedule rebuilding and maintenance.

The serious athlete should be doing this same procedure with blood testing. Blood tests done before something goes wrong can either indicate that all is good, or they can give advanced warning that something needs to change.

If the owner of an earthmoving machine sees slight cracking in the paint, he investigates the possibility of a crack in the steel (earthmoving machines often do things they were not designed to do, causing stresses not anticipated by the manufacturer). If the owner/mechanic detects a crack starting, he doesn't keep working the machine. He puts it straight into the workshop to weld it up.

How often do we see athletes pushing on with their training when cracks start to appear?

Every three months your car goes into the workshop for service. A Cat gets serviced every day. After every day's work, the machine is greased, and a brief check of all oil levels and running gear is carried out by the operator. Fuelling and greasing a machine of the value we're talking about is simply ensuring it's ready for the next day of work.

How often do I have to harp on athletes in my squad about the value of refuelling? How often do my athletes get a massage or chiropractic adjustments?

These machines I'm talking about have working lives of twenty to thirty years. That's a lot of solid hard work. Many are still working well at forty years. How many cars go that long? A taxi works similar hours and generally retires after three years.

The following list summarizes the message:

* Maintenance prolongs the life of the machine and the athlete.

* Little things attended to soon enough don't become major breakdowns.

* Even the toughest machinery in the world will crack if enough pressure is applied (or if it's asked to do what it was not designed to do in the first place).

* Refuelling and regular maintenance prepares the machine and the athlete for the next day or week of work.

A few athletes out there think they're tougher than a Cat. Next time you're driving down the highway and pass some earthmoving gear, stop and then walk up to one of them to see how you measure up. They're built tough to do a tough job. They have no excess trimming; every part of them is functional.

If you put dirty fuel into them, they'll let you down. Think of that next time you buy KFC.

Also, a message for the bigger athletes is that when Cat makes a machine, it gives it a motor big enough to do the job. A D10 bulldozer weighs fifty tons. It has seven hundred horsepower. A D3 weighs eight tons and has sixty-five horsepower.

So when you're out there training, don't pull out the old excuse that another athlete is only sixty kilograms, so you'll never go as fast as that person because you weigh ninety-five kilograms. When God builds humans, he uses a similar scale to Caterpillar. He gives the bigger ones bigger engines. So if your ninety-five kilograms is not all lard, when you hit that next big hill, think of yourself as having seven hundred horsepower. -- If you know what you're worth, then go out and get what you're worth.

Analysis of Statistics and Performance

One of the things that has amazed me in triathlon since '83 and '84, when I first became involved, is the gadgetry that's available now.

It's no secret that the average triathlete is a reasonably successful person in his or her chosen career. There is more disposable income in the pockets of most triathletes to spend on gadgets than the average Aussie battler has to spend on beer and ciggies.

I find it amazing that athletes are out there training with three satellites tracking them and a gadget on their wrists telling them what speed they're travelling, what the temperature is, what their elevation is, and what their exact location on the planet is. Not only that, they're measuring their heart rates, average heart rates, max heart rates, distances travelled, stride lengths, average speeds, and max speeds reached.

The surprising fact is that when they race, none of that bullshit matters at all. How they feel inside has far more impact on their performances than anything else.

Confidence, the ability to focus intently, staying calm under changing conditions, and self-belief are the qualities most likely to determine the outcome on race day. But there is no gadget invented that can measure these things.

Without the qualities listed above, it doesn't matter what elevation you've gained, what your average speed is, or exactly where you are on the planet. The fact is without these qualities, you're f***ed.

So when I ask my athletes for feedback, I want 30 per cent of the feedback to be about physical performance and 70 per cent to be about how they felt during the workout.

I want to know what's going on inside their hearts and heads. The fact that they think about these things and report them to me encourages them to self-examine. I want to know, but most of all, I want them to know how they're feeling.

What we'll learn from this is how to "turn ourselves on" for races. We'll learn what situations to avoid before races. We'll learn how to overrule detrimental thought processes and replace undermining influences with motivating ones.

Most of all, we'll learn more about ourselves as people and athletes.

Understanding the animal we're working with will enable us to tap into the reserves, which sports science just can't measure.

The coach's job is to see the best in humans, who have often not seen the best in themselves.

Synergy—Every Little Thing Is Important

I often laugh when someone copies something we do in training. It rarely works as well for someone else as it does for us. There's always someone looking for the secret.

The secret is that there is no secret. Don't tell anyone. If there was any one factor that causes my athletes to outperform many of their competitors who are actually doing more training, it's synergy.

Often athletes have trained with the squad for a season or two and then decided to move on and do their own thing. Very often these same athletes fail to do equal the performances they had produced when they trained in the squad. Looking from the outside, they're doing almost everything the same.

But that's just it. Almost the same is not the same! The plan we work on has been refined over many years and is still being refined. The success of this plan is a direct result of everything in the plan working together. Lots of little seemingly meaningless things complementing each other.

A good example of this is vitamin C. When nature makes vitamin C, it always packages it with bioflavonoids. In an orange, the bioflavonoids are in the white part just under the skin. Vitamin C without bioflavonoids is far less effective. Pure ascorbic acid (vitamin C) without bioflavonoids is almost ineffective in boosting immune systems and speeding healing. Bioflavonoids are the catalysts that cause vitamin C to do the magic it often does. So when I advise my athletes to get "bio-C," that's exactly what I want them to get. Google bioflavonoids for all the benefits.

When someone starts training with me, I ask him or her to provide a three-day food diary. I want to know what fuel my "formula-one racer" has in its tank. In 80 per cent of cases, some modification is necessary. I also want to know what supplements the person takes, if any. I then advise what I want taken. I don't sell them, but I want my formula-one racers on high-octane fuel.

Usually what happens toward the end of the second month (as long as the athlete has followed the directions to the letter—and if ever in doubt, please ask) is that the athlete comments on being able to train more consistently than ever before. By the end of the third month, the athlete is performing better than ever before and excited about the future. This is partly because all of the blood cells are replaced with new ones over a three-month period. If the new blood cells are being produced from better nutrition, they're better blood cells. So after three months of good nutrition and balanced training, my athlete has a whole new blood supply.

This new blood is capable of carrying oxygen more efficiently. This new blood has no parasites feeding off it because the athlete has wormed himself at the start of each program. In a "hemeview" blood test, you can see the blood cells under a microscope. You can see malformed cells, and you can see the activity level of your white blood cells (your immune system). It's a very interesting study to have a hemeview test and then to have another after three months of good nutrition and balanced training.

Another simple little thing is the confidence level of the athlete. My workouts are structured to build confidence as much as to build fitness. Changing a program around or leaving out a part you don't like is like leaving out part of the jigsaw. I can tell what sort of feelings athletes are experiencing by just reading their e-mails. This is why I get best results in the second season with newer athletes as I get to know them better.

Girls are often better at doing everything to the letter than guys are. Maybe that's why I have had twice as many girls stand on the stage in Hawaii than guys. Doing the little things like core-strength work can make an enormous difference in the last ten kilometres of an Ironman marathon. There's only one way to do core-strength work—that's properly. Even in our squad, I see athletes not taking core-strength work seriously. Sloppy work produces sloppy results.

Visualisation is another really important part of training. See yourself swimming like the best swimmers in the world and cycling like Lance Armstrong. (We'll never have Lance's talent, but we can be as technically good on the bike as he is if we work at it.) I have a picture of myself taken in the Forster Ironman in 97, half-way through the marathon. It's a front-on photo showing perfect form. Last year I was injured for months after a bike fall. As I worked my way back into running, I used that picture as the image of what I wanted to be running like. I refused to limp. I refused to practice poor technique. Every short treadmill run was perfect. I have that photo in my office to help my visualisation. It doesn't have to be a photo of yourself. As long as what you're seeing is perfect.

This message is so important. I have many more examples of the importance of all the little things that contribute to an overall superb performance, but if this instruction gets any longer, you'll lose interest.

Triathlon fitness is as complex as many of nature's miracles. As in nature, every little part is important.

Everything starts by just getting out of bed. When the alarm goes off, just get out right away, without thinking. There's nothing to be gained by thinking about it.

Ulterior Motive

I write training programs for athletes for what they want—a better performance in their next race, their target race, or a series of races over the next season. That's easy to achieve.

When they have been with me for a season, a couple of seasons, or in some cases, many years, I aim for them to be healthier, happier people than when they first contacted me. It's one of the rewards of being a coach, the ability to influence people positively.

Lots of people training for Ironman and even Half Ironman, actually lower their levels of health and/or their levels of self-confidence over a season or two. I don't want that to happen to any of my athletes. I aim for our relationships to be those of healthy growth and personal development.

Optimum performance comes from total health, aerobic efficiency, great technique, and inner joy that comes from loving what you do. You don't have to win the Hawaii Ironman to have all of these attributes. I know some athletes who will never place in a category, but the joy they get from training and racing with such a positive bunch of people adds a huge amount of quality to their lives.

I also know some athletes who are such wankers that they have no time to talk to those who are not as fast as they are. Their favourite subject is themselves. They have a lot to learn. I'm sure, in time, they'll either learn or leave. Either way we'll all be better off.

Total health is not just the absence of illness. This is the spark that people have when living is fun. Anyone training for an Ironman must take nutritional supplements. They must take oil supplements to balance their fat intake to ensure there is enough of the good oils. Recovery feeding is one of the simplest things to get right, but many don't do it well enough. Ironman athletes need more protein than body builders do. Most athletes I meet don't get enough. The greatest mistake most make is they get work-rest balance wrong. Instead of focusing on recovery, they focus on the biggest workload.

An athlete training well, on a good diet, and having adequate rest looks like a thoroughbred at the Melbourne Cup—shiny, healthy hair; strong fingernails; healthy, shiny skin; and a strong, lean body. Last weekend at the Gold Coast Half Ironman race, fewer than 40 per cent of the field looked like this. Too many were too fat. Many were performing way below their potential. Many looked one workout away from their next illness or injury.

Aerobic efficiency—Training at a moderate pace, not racing your mates, gradually building the duration of the workouts, and having enough rest to recover properly will do it every time. The time to impress is race day. Train to race; don't race to train. You'll do a lot less walking in the marathon when you get this right. Don't do too many other activities outside of your training. Ironman Triathlon is a life full of activity. There's no time left for other sports.

Great technique—There is only one way to do something right. Why is it that the best in any field do whatever they do so perfectly. Tiger Woods, Valentino Rossi, and Chris McCormack all have one thing in common: perfect technique. My training philosophy is to practice perfect technique and become fit as a result of that practice. Even online athlete clients in foreign countries can video themselves, put their videos on YouTube, and give me the links. I check their swim or run techniques. I have raced Hawaii eleven times. Everyone I have passed in the final forty kilometres of the bike leg have been pedaling incorrectly, just mashing the pedals. You can never afford to practice sloppy technique. It'll come back when you're at your most tired and despondent.

Inner Joy—We might joke with our friends about smashing each other or destroying our opposition, but the best performances come from athletes who love what they do and are happy inside. To your opposition this may not be apparent. You can be fiercely competitive but still love what you're doing and have respect for your competitors. When you stand at the start line of the biggest races in the world and know that you're racing for the sheer love of it. You're going to do your very best in each leg of them. There's no reason for fear or nerves. It is natural to have some nervous excitement. This is where great performances spring from. Love what you're about to do, and you turn it into fun.

Don't pray for an easy life; pray for the strength to endure a difficult one.

How Much Has Compromise Cost You?

I've just read another biographical book, *Lewis Hamilton: My Story*. I am always reading biographies of sports and business leaders. I take every opportunity to meet successful people.

They all have a common thread: attention to detail. In Lewis Hamilton's story, as with Schumacher, he is totally professional. He attends to every little detail necessary to be the best he can be. When he was first given the chance to drive formula one for McLaren-Mercedes, he introduced himself to every member of the support team and learned everything he could about every aspect of preparing a formula-one racing car. What's surprising is that even at that level, many other drivers don't bother with these things.

During our Sunday afternoon switch-off session. After a physically stressful morning session, we refuel as though we're professional athletes. After a shower, I often have a short sleep, and then we like to go to the movies. While we're there, we become totally absorbed in the film. This is a necessary break from work or training. This switching off is as important as training. It's amazing how many world champions of all sports use this same strategy.

The movie we saw was *Body of Lies* with Russell Crowe and Leonardo DiCaprio. Before we chose that movie, we knew it would be good. Russell Crowe doesn't play in bad films because he doesn't have to. We've seen most of Crowe's movies and have never been disappointed. His energy in every role he plays is amazing. Every detail is covered. I'm sure when his career was young, he would have been pressured to make compromises to simply put food on the table. But Russell's professionalism and his attention to detail is what has moved him to the front of his field.

Much the same way we see people around us making compromises every day, roughness is almost expected amongst tradesmen. When we come across a tradie who does exactly what we expect when we expect it and at a fair price, we almost applaud. The guys who do their jobs without compromising their professionalism, whether it's racing a formula-one car, acting on the world stage, or fixing plumbing, all end up at the top of the heap.

In our sport, whether you race as a professional for prize money or are an age grouper racing for a time or a place in your category, the fewer compromises you make from the perfect plan, the better your results will be. Professionalism is not something reserved for pro athletes. We can all benefit from a more professional approach.

Lewis Hamilton has people who help him with all the little details, but he drives the whole attitude thing with his own approach. Most of us don't have someone to look after our little things, so we have to become good at them ourselves.

Start making lists and checking things off. If all the little things are done, racing the race is easy.

Professionalism is not just a race-day thing; it's an everyday thing. Diet, equipment, technique, rest, refuelling, sleep, and balance—there's your first list. Each of those headings can become another list.

Life never gets easier; you just get stronger.

There's No Such Thing as a Free Lunch

There's always someone looking for an easier way. It doesn't matter what field it's in, shortcutting is happening. We hear stories of age-group athletes taking performance-enhancing drugs. What in the hell for? To be recognised by a handful of people as the winner of some minor category in a sport most of the population don't even notice. Recently my sixteen-year-old son asked me about the benefits of taking creatine. His mates at school were all talking about it. They were playing rugby or rowing for the school. I believe there are high school football players on steroids.

It was difficult to not lecture him. At that age, it's not easy to have a blokes-type conversation. I told him there was no such thing as a free lunch. I pointed out to him that he's naturally quite muscular compared to his mates. He got that way from the seven years he trained at gymnastics. That was seven years of six- to fourteen-hours of training every week. His mates want to build themselves up to be stronger and look better.

No matter what you might take to get some benefit, there's very likely to be a side effect. If a guy has a cortisone injection into his knee or hip so he can play in a big game, what will happen inside that knee or hip joint while he can't feel pain?

In television ads, when we see people taking painkillers, "For when strong pain strikes," chances are a good night's sleep or a big drink of water could cure that strong pain. The patient is not suffering from a deficiency of Advil. The patient more likely suffers from a deficiency of sleep or fluid. The pain may be gone, but the problem still exists.

I recently heard of someone who was considering taking human growth hormone (HGH). I asked about the benefits and what sport he was competing in. No sport; he just trains at the gym. He wanted to lose a bit of body fat and build his muscles up, not to compete but to look good. I believe one of the worst side effects of HGH is the cost. I have to ask, why not just do the work? Live a clean life, eat a good diet, and train hard. How many guys working out down at the local gym are on steroids just to look good.

I believe the benefits of applying yourself and doing as good a job as possible far outweigh the benefits of shortcutting. It appears that satisfaction is underrated these days. I'm sure people have been shortcutting forever, but it seems to be a far greater problem today. Taking the time to do a job well has huge benefits.

When we race an Ironman race, it's not just a one-day event. It's the culmination of four- or five-month's work, patiently putting all the pieces together so that on this one day, we'll be able to use our bodies to the limits. What we feel when we put that plan into action is satisfaction, knowing that we've put it all together and completed the job.

For me it's the most satisfying experience I can have. I guess that's what keeps bringing me back.

When you talk, you are only repeating what you already know. When you listen, you may learn something new.

To Use These Bodies Again, We Have to Look after Them

Thirty of our athletes competed in the WA Ironman in Busselton. It's a beautiful venue for a race, and we all enjoyed ourselves.

It's not uncommon for athletes to get sick after smashing themselves over an Ironman distance race. Often the reason they get sick is simply from not looking after themselves right after the race.

I have found athletes will take any supplement they can lay their hands on in the week before the race. But right after it's over, they'll forget to take their vitamins. Worse than that, they'll eat things they've been denying themselves for months. So they go from "the body is a temple" to "the body is a trash can" almost overnight.

Most of us want to celebrate our performance—have a few drinks, eat some of the foods we've been craving. That's all okay, but how about refuelling the body before letting loose.

Over the years, I've found my body is hungry for essential oils right after a long, hot race. It must be the amount of antioxidants used up during the extended effort.

My usual nutrition plan for right after an Ironman is as follows:

* The day before the race, I make a big pot of salty chicken and vegetable soup to have when I get home. I find small meals every two to three hours is good for a stressed stomach.

* As soon as I finish, I start refuelling with sugar (soft drinks) and a little bit of the food offered at the finish line.

* As soon as I get back to where we're staying, I make a large drink of Endura Opti (about six scoops in about two to three hundred millilitres of water)

* With that Opti drink, I take two thousand milligrams of vitamin C, four capsules of fish oil, one zinc capsule, and two hundred milligrams of CoQ10.

* The supplements above are to quench the free radicals in my system. I find the temperature of my outward breath is reduced within twenty minutes, indicating to me a return to balance. Try this after long, hard workouts.

* The chicken soup is available anytime I get hungry through that first night. I find I have to eat three or four times before breakfast the next day.

* Then the next day can be treated like any other. By that evening, it's okay to start celebrating. Most of the immediate recovery has been done.

This recovery feeding plan has helped me avoid the inevitable illness right after an Ironman. I keep the vitamins and fish oil up for the whole week. I intend to use this body for many more races in the future.

Lack of direction is the problem, not lack of time. We all have twenty-four hours a day.

Getting the Balance Right

There's always someone talking about balance. The type of balance most Ironman triathletes struggle with is the work-to-rest balance. We're almost all obsessed with training. I've known guys who fit in a bike training ride on the morning of their weddings. I've even known some who've taken their bikes on the honeymoon.

As long as enough attention is given to recovery procedures, good food, and good sleep habits, it's possible to do a lot of training in the hours left after work and sleep. This is an area where we do see a few athletes get it wrong. We have to consider our family commitments in the quest for balance in the program.

Remember, a five-year-old kid is only going to be five for a short time. The time spent with him or her at this time is invested in the future. Contrary to what some mums might say, a dad who trains often and races every couple of months is a great role model for that child. Not only is Dad leading by example, he's keeping his mind and body healthy. This makes him a better husband and father. I've known guys who've risen at 3:00 a.m. to fit their training in before the kids get up, still run a very successful business, and win their categories in major races.

If Dad is spending his leisure time at the pool, out on the bike with his mates, or going for a run while the kids ride their bikes along with him, this has to be a better example than Dad and his mates sitting around drinking a carton of beer every weekend.

The fulfilment of our spirits is one of the great side benefits of training and racing Half Ironman and Ironman races. It's the satisfaction gained by training for something that we know is going to be hard but beating it anyway. That uplifting of the spirit through being superbly fit and facing the challenges we've set before ourselves makes us more alive than many.

If it was easy, they wouldn't call it the Ironman. We live dumbed-down lives—they even put warning signs on hammers nowadays. Our society watchdogs have excused away just about every stupid act a person could commit by giving it a syndrome name.

The overachievers have to break out and do something a bit dangerous, something exciting and challenging, just to save going mad. Any child who has a dad or mum who train and compete in Ironman-type events is truly lucky. Any woman who has a husband who spends his leisure time cycling, running, and swimming and who has a passion for fitness is far luckier than many of her peers.

Passionate people produce. That simple slogan sums up why most of the members of my squad are overachievers in all parts of their lives. The passion ignited in every training session sends the athletes off to their workplaces on a high.

Problems are solved more easily than by their sluggish workmates. Relationships are more exciting because the athletes' self-esteem is high. A person with a high self-esteem has more to give. His or her needs are already filled.

All these benefits are available to the athlete with his or her life in balance. You'll know if you have it in balance. Don't take notice of the criticism that may come from someone whose life is empty. You have the energy to help those sad people find something to build their passion.

I'm not telling you it's going to be easy; I'm telling you it's going to be worth it.

Persistence Prevails When All Else Fails

Over the past twenty years, I have seen so many talented athletes give up on their dreams about one season too early. They've let the dream slip away when they were so close. A little bit more perseverance was all that was needed.

The talent was there and the skills were usually well developed. They just needed a little more refining over another year. Maybe it's the Generation Y thing, where young people want to go straight to the top without doing the groundwork. But it's not just Gen Y. Athletes of all ages start out with a list of goals to achieve, and many run out of commitment before the journey has been completed.

I'm as guilty of this as much as anyone. Over the years, I have started seven businesses from scratch and worked really hard to make everyone of them successful. But once they had reached a level where things were running smoothly and profitably, I lost interest and went off on another project. It seems I like the struggle to get there, but once I'm almost there and the struggle is done, I look for something else to struggle at.

It takes discipline to stick at something and to see it through to completion. We must have a clearly defined path and definite goals to reach along the way—things to tick off the list. It's also important to share our long-term goals with someone we trust. This makes them harder to abandon.

There's a great story of a Sicilian family that makes me feel good every time I recall it: the Casella family's success story. The founder and his wife arrived in Australia with nothing in 1936. They started a winery near Griffith. At the time, Australians hardly drank wine; it was a beer-drinking country. They sold their wine from the back of their truck to other immigrants around the area, and the business is still run by the family.

As the business grew, they looked at export markets for their budget-priced, good-tasting wines. I first tasted their wines in Hawaii a few years ago. They have become the largest supplier of imported wines in the USA, with their Yellowtail brand. The family business exports eight million cases of wine annually. Last year the sales reached 426 million dollars, but profit had fallen to 40 million with the economic downturn. This story makes me feel good inside. The persistence over three generations and seventy years has turned a "back of the truck" business into an international success story.

Our dreams may not be as grand as the Casella family story, but our personal athletic journeys can be much grander than we ever imagined if we have plans and if we stick to them. There are going to be times when the going gets tough. Illness, injury, and loss of motivation can all slow progress for a while.

But getting back on track after a setback is the one single thing that can determine whether we're there when the champagne is being poured. Every athlete has setbacks at some time. Read the biographies of champions; they're full of setbacks being overcome.

I have found that when athletes have an unsatisfying race, the next major race they do is a ripper. I've seen major breakthroughs come from the fuel of disappointment.

Surround yourself with people who know your worth. You don't need many people to be happy, just a few real ones who appreciate you for who you are.

The Limiter

Whether we're lining up for our first long-course race or our fortieth Ironman, the common limiter is our minds. The human mind has evolved into a mostly pessimistic, fear-driven control tower. The early humans had to be fearful. Those who were not wary of what might go wrong were probably eaten by someone else or something else, before they had a chance to breed.

To reach breeding age in the ancient world, a human had to manage to avoid being eaten or killed by all sorts of things. The cautious ones made it. So our modern human has been bred from a long line of very cautious players. Is it any wonder that when we train or race, our minds go through every possible scenario that could go wrong?

Successful athletes have this chatter going on as well, but they have become skilled in overruling the cautious voices, to an extent. Successful athletes are still cautious, but they don't dwell on the negatives. We meet optimists in every walk of life. These gifted people always see what's possible, not what will go wrong. They're very aware of what can go wrong, but they apply their attention to driving what can go right.

It's possible to learn to see the brighter side of every situation. It's much easier to learn this skill in the company of other established optimists. "You can't fly like an eagle if you're surrounded by turkeys." Seek out the company of people who lift your expectations. If you're stuck with a pessimistic group, be the one who drives the optimism. Every group that lacks positive leadership is a group waiting for a strong leader. You don't have to be physically strong to lead; you just have to have a strong mind and attitude, and you have to lead by example.

I was training for my forty-first Ironman. I completed my training sessions after the squad had done their sessions. During the squad session, I am the driver of spirit, and I talk people through difficult turbo sessions. I lead the group through core-strength sessions, but when I get to do my own turbo session or longer swim session, I have that little voice chatting away in my head, trying to convince me that cutting something short will be okay.

In thirty years of training for Ironman races, I have had my ups and downs, my periods of lower motivation, and my times of mental mastery. Training for an Ironman is an exercise in mastering the voices, dominating our own self-talk. One of the reasons we do regular one hundred-kilometre time trials is to give athletes the chance to face who they really are. To give each athlete the chance to master one square metre of this planet.

To get good results in a race that takes all day, we have to have control of what happens in one square metre at a time. Our thoughts will race to other things outside our square metre more than one hundred times during a one hundred-kilometre time trial. In a full Ironman race, it could be one thousand times that we have to bring our thoughts back into our square metre. We have to go into the race with a strategy that we can use to bring our thoughts back to the important job at hand.

When I train with a group, I still have to control my thoughts, avoid comparing myself with others, and focus on efficient technique, especially when tired. But when I train alone, I really have to work at it. I would say that I spend more energy focussing on maintaining the right attitude than I do on the goal or the outcome at the end of the session. If we can get into the zone of the most productive attitude and hold it, the outcome will look after itself.

I encourage my athletes to count their revs during intervals on the bike. We've found that counting revs can smooth out pedalling technique and actually produce more power than watching the power meter. Watching the power meter is focusing on the outcome; counting revs is focusing on the process. That last line is the most valuable training and racing tip I could give anyone. When I race, I count revs the whole way; I don't count any specific number. I just count to the next sign, the next post, the next anything you pick.

I expect to lose control of my thoughts many times during a race, but I'll go back to counting strokes in the swim, counting revs on the bike, or counting steps on the run. My strategy is to go back to counting as soon as my thoughts drift to another competitor or as soon as they drift to a finish time. If I can manage to focus on the process as much as possible, my outcome will be the best I can produce.

One day as a tiger is worth a thousand as a sheep.

Testing—What We Learn

Testing is part of the plan. We train, we test, we train, and we test again. A big part of the testing program is the psychological side. We become so used to timed efforts, that the sight of the stopwatch no longer puts any fear into us. There was a time when I brought the stopwatch out, and people in the squad would start making all sorts of excuses as to why they would not be ready for a timed effort. You don't have to be tapered and fresh to swim a timed effort or do a functional threshold power (FTP) test on the bike.

Testing is an important part of training. It's just part of being an athlete. In fact, most of us are living lives that require us to be tested regularly in our work environments. If we can remove the fear of being judged from the testing procedure, most of us will actually perform better.

When I test my athletes, I choose a test that's not so long that it'll impact the athletes continued training rhythms. The swim test I like to use is 6 x (100m free + 50m band). It's a nine hundred metre-swim time trial that includes 300m of band (around the ankles). This test shows me the quality of the catch and hold portion of the swim stroke. Placing the band around the ankles forces the swimmer to catch water. All the fancy drills are of little value if the athlete is not grabbing water. The swimmers who reduce their test time by two minutes over a season usually take five minutes off their Ironman swim time.

We regularly do two types of bike tests. The FTP test, using a power meter. I usually get the guys to warm up and go as hard as they can for twenty minutes, and then I record the average power. This is a good guideline for me to set intensity figures for interval work. The other test that everyone in the squad can use, even those without power meters, is the one hundred-kilometre time trial. I've chosen the figure of one hundred kilometres because it's too hard for most to ride at their anaerobic threshold but not long enough to leave the athlete with too much fatigue buildup. It's a closer test to the requirements of the Ironman athlete.

The guys do full dress rehearsals in the one hundred-kilometre time trials: aero helmets, race wheels, and race clothing. All this is important. We don't want anything new on race day, so the monthly one hundred-kilometre time trial is treated like a race. It gives the guys race experience without the cost of entering a formally organised race.

Your life is your garden; your thoughts are the seeds. If your life isn't awesome, you've been watering the weeds.

Hard Work Can Override Talent Levels

Talent is not all that important.

I've heard a lot of lazy people excuse themselves for not setting serious goals and not training conscientiously, because they have decided that they don't have enough talent to be worthy of setting big goals.

Then on the other hand, I've seen athletes work hard at all aspects of their sport and overcome all sorts of obstacles along the way. And then they amaze themselves and all those around them with how much talent they have uncovered.

My observation is that the greatest talent an endurance athlete can have is tenacity and attention to the little things.

Flexibility: Anyone who spends a bit of time each day working on flexibility can improve. And the amazing coincidence is that the best swimmers in my squad are more flexible that the poorer swimmers. The same applies to the best runners in the squad. Stretching is important for freedom of movement and, most of all, lack of muscular tension while performing.

Strength: A friend of mine did his Ph.D. on the strength gains with weight training possible in men over sixty. At the time, I was a lot younger and was impressed by the gains made by these old guys. In a group of runners, he increased their muscle mass and overall strength by a significant percentage over an eight- to ten-week period. If you are strong, you not only perform better but also avoid so many of the injuries that your competitors will suffer.

Body weight: There have been studies made on the possible performance gains per kilogram of weight loss. There is so much to gain by keeping yourself at close to race weight through your preparation. You don't have to be skinny, but on the other hand, you don't want to carry the weight of a small child on your belly. Losing weight is easy; you just have to want to.

Everyone I have asked to drop dairy, wheat, and sugar from his or her diet, now has a trim, healthy-looking athlete's body. With this simple eating plan, you never need to be hungry. You can eat as much as you like. As long as none of it is wheat, dairy, or sugar. This simple plan asks you to have 50 to 60 per cent of your diet as vegetables. No one needs to be fat.

Training intensity: Most athletes I've seen become discouraged and drop out of the sport are the ones who race their training sessions, regularly turning aerobic rides and runs into time trials or races with their training partners. Aerobic work needs to be much easier than race pace. Intervals and run-speed work need to be much harder than race pace. Time trials need to be done regularly, and these are at race pace. Know the difference between training and racing.

Training volume: A beginner cannot step straight up to the workload that a seasoned athlete can handle. Early years should be spent laying the foundations for future training blocks. It's no secret that there is a relationship between the volume of training and performance.

The more you do, usually the faster you become. It's not as simple as that, but as an athlete develops, he or she can handle more. This allows for greater aerobic development. But it's also a trap. Doing more will not make you faster if you don't recover from it. So for every increase in volume, there needs to be an equal increase in the attention to recovery procedures.

Recovery feeding: By conscientiously sticking to a recovery drink like Endura Opti after every session, the new athlete gradually becomes leaner and more muscular over six months to a year. It's amazing how much muscle development occurs doing mainly aerobic, endurance-type training.

Endurance athletes need more protein than body builders. The ratio of one-part protein to four-parts carbohydrate is just right to replenish muscle glycogen levels and rebuild muscle tissue. This is an area where you have the chance to "lock away" the gains from each workout.

Have faith in the plan. I've known a lot of athletes who are always researching the latest thing, whether it's the latest nutritional supplement or the latest training idea on a triathlon forum. The secret is not out there waiting to be discovered. Have a look around at the most successful athletes in your squad or club. They have usually already discovered the secret.

It's turning up every session. It's doing the session just the way the coach has set it. It's going easy when you're asked to. It's giving everything when it's time to go hard. It's training when the weather is bad. It's feeding immediately after each session and replenishing everything the body has used.

It's not searching outside the squad for the secret. It's not buying all the latest gadgets to measure your performance. It's not downloading everything on Strava. It's not giving yourself discounts in training sessions. It's not racing your mates in training. It's not doing speed work before you have a base built.

If you train smart and do more things right than your mates, you will never get injured, and you'll continue to improve over many years.

Big mistakes I see athletes outside my squad make are not doing enough low-intensity development work and doing intense speed work sessions way before they have a base built. All distance triathlons are endurance events. The greatest requirement is aerobic capacity. This has to be built along with conditioning of the body before speed work is started.

The right blend of technique work and aerobic-development work will cause the athlete to actually race faster than speed work done prematurely. Giving speed work to unconditioned athletes is like playing Russian roulette.

Sometimes the bad things that happen to us put us directly on the path to the best things that will ever happen to us.

You Don't Have to Get Injured

I see far too many athletes either recovering from an injury or counting the productive weeks of training between injuries. So many of them see injury as part of the game. This should not be the case. Athletes should be able to enjoy their training as an escape from the other, more stressful parts of their lives. I have identified several mistakes I see athletes making that cause injuries, and all can be avoided.

The athlete who trains with several different groups: I personally know some athletes who swim with one squad, run track sessions with another group, and do bike intervals with another group. Then these same athletes get together on weekends and do adventure-type workouts, which are often quite tiring. And even though they are doable, they leave the athlete too exhausted to train effectively for several days.

By training under several coaches, no one single coach is fully aware of the fatigue levels the athlete is carrying or the development level (background) of the athlete. As a consequence, the athlete is often given whatever the rest of the group is doing, instead of a workload tailored for the athlete's individual needs at the time.

Training in a heavily fatigued state at too high an intensity is one of the causes of what many call a torn calf or torn hamstring, when in fact, it's just an exhausted body saying, "Enough; no more."

The driven athlete who subscribes to the "more is better" theory: This sport attracts Type A personalities. If you look around a squad of successful athletes, most are leaders in their fields. Most have the ability to fit more into a life than the average person does. They get up early, and they fit everything in, sometimes at the expense of quality rest. This group often has the "harder is better" or "more is better" mentality.

I have these sort of athletes come into my squad. I reduce the volume of work they have done previously, and they miraculously drop an hour off their Ironman time.

A lot of hard training has been wasted by athletes who have not balanced their lives with adequate rest. Unfortunately, these same athletes can suffer regular minor injuries because their bodies never recover enough before they're loaded again. Once again their bodies are crying out, "Enough; I can't take any more."

The athlete who is too busy to find time to stretch: In many cases, this athlete simply does not see any value in doing anything that does not raise the heart rate. A body that doesn't have the necessary flexibility to operate through its full range of movement is, first thing, not be able to perform at 100 per cent of its potential. The next obstacle encountered by the inflexible athlete is loss of correct body alignment, as muscles work against each other trying to perform. It's like working with a handbrake on.

Your body was designed to operate freely, without opposing muscles inhibiting the movement of the working muscles. Under this sort of tension, something has to give. Some part of you will grind to a halt or, worse, tear or break.

The athlete who hates core strength work: Some athletes in my squad thought I was picking on them because I had pointed out that they didn't do their core-strength work properly. We don't do core strength work to have a showy six pack. It's nice when it happens, but that's not the goal. Without adequate core strength, achieving 100 per cent of your potential is simply not possible. This is one of the little things that can multiply out to a twenty-minute improvement in an Ironman marathon.

It's one of the small factors that allow you to ride 180 kilometres in the aero position without suffering backache. So if you have no back problems in a long, wetsuit swim, then you ride 180 kilometres in the aero position without any back pain, and then you run 42 kilometres holding a good posture, I guarantee you'll have a satisfying result.

Enough injuries can be attributed to poor flexibility and lack of core strength. A book could be written on the subject. The obvious question is, Why wait until you're injured before you start doing these exercises as rehabilitation, when you can do them as prevention?

The athlete who sees little value in swim-technique or run-technique sessions: I have put specific, run- or swim-technique sessions on for the squad. The amazing thing is how so many of the athletes who need it most don't attend them. If you are going to do something, it makes sense to do it properly. Good technique prevents injuries. But an amazing side benefit is that it's faster, particularly when you're tired. Most of the athletes I work with are training for half or full Ironman events. In both cases, the run is started in a fairly fatigued state.

We have to train to run when we're approaching exhaustion. If we have only ever practiced perfect technique, that's what we'll produce on race day. A serious athlete can never afford to practice anything other than perfect technique. Good technique is efficient. Efficient movement is far less likely to injure an athlete, no matter how tired he becomes.

The athlete should not become injured

*   if the training program is written to suit the training age of the athlete,

*   if every session has a purpose not guided by peer pressure,

*   if the athlete has good flexibility,

*   if the athlete has good core strength, and

* if the athlete learns good technique in each sport and practices perfect technique in every session.

The person who says it cannot be done should not interrupt the person doing it.

To Produce Your Best Ironman, You Need to Aim at Becoming the Complete Man

It usually takes a disappointing performance before athletes totally commit to a training plan that will take them to their potential. I have seen discounting occurring in just about every week I have been coaching. That's what I have seen in my own squad, and they're seen as dedicated trainers by many other athletes outside the squad.

The athlete who wasn't completely committed to the diet plan and who raced with two to three extra kilograms around his waist was giving himself a handicap. The guys who got out of the pool early on several occasions or slept in and totally missed sessions were discounting. In each training group, there's always someone who does everything, is always early for sessions, and does every core exercise and every stretch properly. These are the guys who stand on the podium most often.

Reaching your potential in this sport is not a one-season project. It takes years to develop the physiology necessary to perform at your aerobic threshold for a whole day. If you don't achieve what you're aiming at in the first three or four Ironman races, it's not time to give up yet. If you really do have a strong goal, and you have not yet achieved it, you have to re-evaluate your approach.

The post race autopsy is a truly valuable part of the plan. It's so important for the athlete to analyse the performance honestly and write a race report. It doesn't matter if he doesn't post it on the forum, as long as he writes it and has his coach review it. There is so much we can learn from a less satisfying race. Too often the athlete has trained really well, indicating a better performance than he or she delivers on race day.

Often the race analysis will identify what went wrong and where it went wrong. So often it's a psychological issue, a moment when something triggers a switch from doing the job to all of a sudden it being much harder. I've seen athletes blame fuel or a bit of a cough or a sniffle they had the day before. I've seen athletes not be able to stomach the same drinks they used in all their training rides and time trials. The problem is not in the stomach; it's often in the head.

Sadly, this problem can't be solved for months, not really solved until it's tested in another race situation under the sort of pressure we put on ourselves. After a psychological problem like this has been identified, I often prescribe special workouts for that individual. His own special tests, tasks designed to cause self-doubt, take the athlete out of his comfort zone. The only way to overcome a bit of a soft underbelly is to be pushed into a situation where you're confronted with a "do or do not" decision.

Honesty in the post-race evaluation is the most important element. Back slapping and congratulations for mediocre performances don't help anyone. I've seen guys congratulated for dismal performances, guys who've really been beaten by the course. I have been one of them. My own first Ironman was in Hawaii in 1986. I was sick in the week before the race and had not prepared as well as I should have. The course beat me, and I was embarrassed when people congratulated me. I'd walked half the run, totally beaten.

I encourage athletes to set daring goals. Easy, soft goals will not cause athletes to have to stretch; to grow; or to become stronger, better people. But when setting daring, big goals, they have to be backed up with a total athletic approach. Diet, strength, flexibility, recovery, and balance all need to be part of the plan. There's no point talking it up and then not backing it up. It makes you look silly.

When you do everything you can as well as you can, you don't need the applause. You don't need the back slapping. You have that respect for yourself. It takes courage to do the right thing day in, day out. Early mornings and rainy days, any fool can train when fresh. It takes small amounts of courage to keep stepping up to the block and fitting in all the little things, the pieces of the puzzle.

Invest that courage, and earn respect. The respect of those who know you and the respect you feel for yourself when you don't let yourself down.

A focused mind is one of the most powerful forces in the universe.

Pain Tolerance—Are You Born with It, or Do You Develop It?

My mother once had a fall while working in the garden. I picked her up from the hospital the next day, and she was sitting in a wheelchair outside the doors. I thought I'd have to help her up into my truck, but she stood up and walked straight up to the truck, grabbed the handle above the door, opened it, and then pulled herself up into the seat. She showed me her doctor's report.

She'd had a fractured seventh rib, a fractured radius bone in her wrist, and a badly bruised knee (six inches above and below her knee was black and blue). When I dropped her off at home, I gave her a hug, without thinking about it. She winced a bit, as it had hurt her ribs. She's eighty-six years old. I called in to see her a week later, and she was out working in her garden. I surprised her by walking up behind her as she was rolling up the hose on the hose reel. It was hard to believe she had fractured wrist or rib. She's didn't take any painkillers.

My dentist told me last year that I have a high pain threshold, because twice I have gone to sleep while he's done root-canal work on my teeth. I just zone out and let him do his job. I guess my mum just puts pain aside and gets on with the job.

My daughter gave birth to her fourth child in the shower at home. She went in for a shower before going to the hospital, and the baby came along. Do we have some sort of special talent for tolerating pain, or is it simply attitude? My wife was doing an equestrian cross-country event, when she was thrown from her horse. She had dislocated her finger but remounted the horse and finished the course. She didn't even realise she'd dislocated it until someone pointed it out when she finished. She has raced fifteen Ironman races.

I have done lots of different types of manual work over the years, and it's quite natural to have a bit of skin off somewhere on me at any one time. Right now I'm renovating another house and have a couple of deep scratches on one arm, a fairly big bruise on my hand, and a cut across my calf. All of these minor injuries had hurt at the time, but within seconds, I was back concentrating on what I was doing.

I have had guys in my squad get out of the pool and find an ice pack after a hand clash with a swimmer in the next lane. These things simply happen in squad sessions. I wonder if the ice-pack guys actually feel pain worse than a tradie on the tools, or if it's such an event in their lives they feel they have to focus on it for a while.

I have often said that some boys got too many hugs while they were growing up. In my family, if we had a fall and got gravel rash, my dad poured kerosene on it. If we stood on a nail, he poured kerosene on it. I honestly had never seen a Band-Aid until I was fourteen. We just had a torn-up piece of old sheet as a bandage if the wound was deep. I think a lot of kids had a Band-Aid on themselves too much of their youth.

I am suggesting that pain tolerance is a type of conditioning and part of the process in preparing an athlete for tough endurance events. I suggest that the athletes who line up for Ironman Melbourne, for Ironman Port Macquarie, and other races start to relive some of their painful injuries and visualise themselves handling these situations in a way that will make them proud of themselves.

In order to be proud of yourself for being tough, you have to develop a respect for tough people. I believe the first step is to select a role model you admire for his or her sheer toughness. Toughness and resilience are very similar characteristics.

For me to respect Ironman athletes, they have to be able to handle whatever comes along in training and on race day. They have to control emotions. The day is full of highs and lows. The tough athletes keep moving forward regardless of how they're feeling. If you're going to surrender, to give up the fight, step aside and allow the athletes still racing a clear path to the finish line. I don't believe you inherit a high tolerance for pain. It's like courage. You're not born with it; you choose to have it.

Spectacular success is preceded by spectacular, though invisible, mental preparation.

What's Missing in Our Plan?

We do all the swim workouts, we ride all the miles, and we wear out a couple of pairs of shoes a year. Yet our times are static. A year of training and we turn in roughly the same times.

What's going wrong?

1. Are we getting the balance of intensity right? Remember that the easy stuff should be done easy, and the hard stuff should be done hard. I've seen so many athletes doing the easy stuff harder than it needs to be done, and then they are too short of fuel or too tired to do the hard efforts hard enough. The bulk of our training is conditioning, which needs to be done easy enough so we bounce back from it easily. At an easy pace, we can get more hours into a week, and more hours equal better conditioning. Too much training at "race pace" is going to eventually stick you on the old training pace, and it'll never change.

2. Are we prepared to do more hours than our competitors? There's a limit to the number of hours of training our bodies can handle. Too many training hours lead to overtraining. But there are hours we can put in that make us better prepared than our competitors are, without wearing ourselves out. Home cook bulk quantities of wholesome foods that we can use when

we're short of time through the week. Stretching costs us nothing in recovery, but it pays off later. A flexible body moves with less restriction than a tight, inflexible one. You may not have the funds or the time to have a massage every day like a Tour de France cyclist, but you can loosen up muscles after each workout in a few minutes with self-massage. What about skill-building drills? Most drills are not physically demanding, but an athlete with perfect technique will always perform better than an equal athlete with poor technique does. This applies to all three sports.

3. Do we spend any time working on our concentration skills? Simply learning to live in the moment can pay huge dividends during races. This is best practiced during timed efforts. In the pool, become aware of which thoughts help you go faster (often it's the very simplest of thoughts). Just becoming aware is advantageous. Running has been described as moving meditation. Become aware of this. Calculating splits and keeping track of other athletes in a race is not the best formula for success for most athletes. Some work okay with this method, but most work best limiting their thoughts to their own square metre. These skills can be learned and practiced during other activities. If you're mowing the lawn, just focus on mowing the lawn. You'll be amazed how quickly the time slips by. If you're peeling potatoes, just think about peeling

potatoes. It'll help heaps on race day, and all those potatoes are good training fuel.

4. Most of us are not born with courage. We choose to have it. It doesn't have to be as extreme as entering a dark building with the possibility of armed enemy soldiers lurking inside. It takes small amounts of courage almost every day to stay on your chosen course. It takes a small amount of courage to push yourself through that hard set in the pool. You'll see examples of people choosing to miss half of it or sitting one out. At moments like that, don't let that little voice in your head tell you it's okay to miss one out. Courage is overruling that little voice in your head. How many times has that little voice changed the course of your life? The more times you overrule that little voice, the weaker it becomes and the stronger you become. Look forward to challenging that little voice.

5. A great coach once said, "Ability is nothing to be proud of, having talent is just luck, effort is something worth being proud of." Are you putting in the sort of effort that you're proud of? Or are you just going through the motions? Lots of athletes are out there training, but when they should be giving their best, many are saving themselves. There are very few things we have the chance to do, which will give us the feeling of satisfaction that giving everything in a workout can give. Learning to chase that feeling will become a

habit. That habit carries over into races. Rather than worrying too much about what other athletes are doing on race day, try chasing that feeling of satisfaction you've experienced in training.

6. Big goals produce big results. Big goals are broken down into small steps. Most athletes I've met who have not advanced at the rate they should have, have either not set big enough goals or not believed in themselves enough to truly own those goals. The best way to build self-belief is to set small, achievable goals often. As these goals are achieved, an increased level of self-belief starts to build. Bigger, more daring goals can be made. This talent comes easy to some; others need to work on it. It's the basic, first step to success.

Lack of equipment is seldom a cause for disappointing triathlete performances. In fact, in many cases, athletes are over-equipped. So often the athlete looks outside of himself for the reason why he hasn't performed. Buying more gear will not make up for poor use of time or lack of commitment.

Everyone has two choices. We're either full of love or full of fear.

Seconds Count

Every second counts. This is the second weekend in a row that I've been timekeeper and watched the guys time trialling at Walloon. Even though, in the newsletter, I wrote about the differences between the faster riders and the slower ones, I see the same little differences occurring.

Whether it's a race or a time trial in training, every second counts. A few seconds of rolling "too big a gear" and not shifting back to a gear where the rider is most efficient, costs seconds. Sitting up and coasting without the pedals turning while drinking is giving away more seconds.

Saving seconds is a winner's habit. Winners don't waste seconds. They do everything as efficiently as possible. You can't waste seconds in training and expect to be efficient when you race. Saving seconds is a habit. Work on developing that habit.

In races, there are so many seconds wasted by people around you. It's almost an unfair advantage to not waste any yourself. Watching an Ironman transition area can help you to formulate your next race plan. In the swim to bike transition (T1) the high number of people doing a complete change of clothes after a wetsuit swim is amazing. It's possible to gain a hundred places in T1 by simply running in, taking off your wetsuit, and running out to your bike. What else needs to be done in there?

For your next race, make saving seconds your mission for the day. We often talk of nine-hour, thirty-minute Ironman being 570 efficient minutes or ten hours being six hundred efficient minutes. It doesn't matter what time you end up with; it's a combination of all the efficient minutes added to the inefficient ones.

The strategies of racing efficient minutes or saving seconds are psychologically easier to handle than racing for a time or a position. Focusing on the process is a far better strategy than focusing on the outcome.

Saving seconds can be a game you play when you train. It can become a habit. It's already a habit of very successful people.

One day you'll wake up, and there'll be no more time to do all the things you wanted to do. Do them now.

Where should We Start to Build an Athlete?

Recently at the Gold Coast Marathon, we stood at the twenty-two kilometre mark and watched everyone from the leaders back to where the attention seekers started coming through. The people with silly hats, costumes, and so on. One guy (a sushi eater) ran the marathon backward, carrying a big flag. Another one from the same place wore all-white compression tights from ankle to wrist. He had shoulder-length hair (Japan's answer to Fabio, the most beautiful man in the world).

Apart from the attention seekers, the most noticeable thing about the runners struggling to break five hours was their running techniques. They were terrible. Most were wasting so much energy that I have to wonder how they train for a marathon.

As mentioned earlier, when new athletes join my squad, the first thing I want from them is clear goals. Their goals supply the energy that drives the consistency. The next thing I want is a three-day food diary. I have to know what they're eating and when they're eating it. Everything they'll become is going to be determined by their diets and how well they absorb the nutrients.

The next step is to start a steady build-up of aerobic work. During that process, I examine their swim, bike, and run techniques. Their backgrounds and past experiences usually show in their techniques. Some are good at one sport but need work on the other two. Some need to start from scratch in all three sports.

The best way to start an athlete is by building technical skills first and then gradually developing fitness. What was evident at the Gold Coast was that many had never learned how to run. They'd just gone out and trudged around the streets for who knows how many miles and worn out their shoes.

While watching members of the public swim at the Yeronga pool where we train, it's pretty obvious that many have never had a swimming lesson. They just grind up and down the pool, often using twice the energy necessary.

If time trial times indicate a weakness in online athletes, I'll ask them to video themselves swimming or running. Then they post the videos on YouTube for me to analyse. So, even online athletes can benefit from a coach's feedback.

The amazing thing about most runners is that when they were little kids, they moved efficiently. Then as they grew up, they developed bad posture habits and poor walking techniques that carried over to their running. If you don't walk technically well, you will not run technically well.

Many of the running injuries suffered by back-of-the-pack runners could be avoided by building good core strength and by maintaining good flexibility. After years of getting used to bad posture, good posture might feel wrong or strange. A good physio (with a sports background) can help point out what's wrong way before an injury occurs.

Swimming poorly makes covering the distance take a long time, and it can also injure your shoulders. Running poorly, with poor core strength and bad posture, can cause terrible discomfort, very slow times, and almost certain injury if you persist.

A runner in the top 10 per cent of the field runs tall and relaxed. He leads each stride with his knee, not with his foot. He lands with his foot right below his hip and pushes the ground back. He has enough core strength, so it is no trouble to resist gravity. His foot is on the ground for the shortest possible time. He hardly makes a sound on the road. His eyes are focused on a point about one to two hundred metres ahead.

I see the same thing when I've watched an Ironman race. The way cyclists will grind a far too high gear and then be unable to run after. Often climbing fairly steep hills in the aero position, these are not the guys doing the fastest times.

Any athletes starting a new sport should focus most of their attention on learning how to do it right before worrying about going fast. Those who can resist human nature or testosterone and get it right, before increasing miles, will progress through the sport faster than the ego-driven athletes.

~~Good things come to those who wait.~~
Good things come to those who work
their asses off and never give up.

Knowledge or Energy—Is There a Secret?

Triathletes have a few things in common, more than the fact that they all like to swim, bike, and run. A great many of them have an insatiable thirst for knowledge. They're constantly reading articles in magazines, researching on the net, and always looking for the secret.

I think one of the factors involved here is that most of the triathletes I meet are into Ironman events, and Ironman triathletes are usually overachievers in every part of their lives. Most people I've trained are at the top of their fields at work or are in jobs that serve a purpose so that they can excel in some other field.

If there is a secret, I believe its passion. Passion and energy are so closely linked, I'm not sure if they're actually different things. Passionate people find a way to get what they want. They find what they need to get the job done. If I were able to give my kids a gift that would help them make it to the top of whatever fields they chose, it would be passion.

Knowledge, on the other hand, is essential in putting together the detailed plans necessary to make a recreation like Ironman triathlon fit around a life— nutritional knowledge, physiological knowledge, and the complex technical knowledge needed to master three sports. I've known a lot of athletes who have let themselves down by becoming obsessed with accumulating knowledge at the cost of just going out there and doing it.

I know a guy who has three university degrees, yet he averages staying in a job for about a year at a time. As soon as it's time for the company to trim out the dead wood, sadly, they let him go. The guy is lazy. Between jobs he has worked with me on a renovation project I was doing. He only worked for me once. He has knowledge coming out of his ears. He's an expert at quite a few things, but he can't hold a job. I won't even use him as a labourer.

The wealthiest man I know started out as a school teacher. He has energy and passion that he's directed into making a fortune. Another mate was a bread vendor. He's now an international landscape designer and builder of the world's best resort gardens. His passion and energy separates him from most other people in his field. Both of these men use other people's knowledge and drive it with their own energy.

If there's a secret to success in business, in Ironman triathlon, it's energy.

It's the energy to get out there and do it, while the others are researching it or talking about it. The guys and girls who've come through my squad have moved past "technically better." More gifted athletes have one thing in common. Energy or passion that has them there when it's raining, when it's cold, or when the wind's blowing a gale, always loving what they're doing and gradually gaining inches on their competitors.

You will never out-train a bad diet.

Altitude or Attitude?

I recently had a conversation with a triathlete who will most likely be embarrassed to read this. I won't mention any names or places. In the course of a ten-minute conversation, he used negative self-talk so smoothly, so habitually, that he'd given himself all the reasons why he couldn't perform in a race.

He was totally unaware of consequences of the words coming out of his mouth. He was a nice, normal guy with no physical handicaps. He had the time to train, and he had the equipment. Yet every conversation we had, he offered more reasons why he couldn't be competitive.

Training at altitude is a tactic used by athletes in many sports to improve oxygen uptake. When they return to sea level, they have a greater ability to absorb oxygen, and as a result, they can go farther and faster than their competitors. Now, the gains made by training at altitude are not huge, but they've been proven to be significant enough to make a difference.

Changing a habit of negative self-talk in an athlete could bring about a huge change in performance far greater than spending a couple of months at five thousand feet.

It's a natural thing to have self-talk going on in our minds most of the time. One of the main benefits of meditation is to either silence, or at least control, the self-talk so that it's not a distraction. Average athletes can gain a lot by just becoming aware of the self-talk they use.

The next step is to have some constructive self-talk ready to run with as soon as the negative stuff starts. The next time you make an excuse for not doing what you set out to do, and the moment you feel yourself finding an excuse (excuses are simply reasons to fail), turn on empowering self-talk.

Many of us have spent our lives coming up with all the reasons to fail and have not been aware of what we're doing. It's time to take responsibility for what happens. If you didn't get the job done, I don't want to hear the reasons why. I want to see you taking action to do it better next time. Not succeeding first time around is not failing.

Failing is accepting it as final and coming up with a reason why you can't do it. Not succeeding is gaining experience. Gaining experience makes a positive outcome much more likely next time you go into the arena.

There's a huge benefit to be gained by attempting something that you may not be successful at on the first, second, or third attempt. Each time you start the next attempt, you have more experience and more determination.

A- An athlete, hardened by the disappointment of several unsuccessful attempts is a formidable force to be faced by the opposition. The "I will not be beaten" attitude is the greatest asset an athlete can have.

Altitude can help, but attitude is the king.

Are You a Man of Action?

How quickly are you able to convert directions and advice into action?

Successful athletes have many common traits, such as converting directions to actions, quickly and efficiently. Recently, one of my athletes told me of a sore calf, which was still tight two days after a long run. Not torn, just tight and making its presence felt. My advice to him was to try Jiang, my acupuncturist, who I've been using and sending athletes to for twelve years.

One hour later I had an e-mail from him telling me he had an appointment the next day. Now that's the type of action that gets results. No hesitation and no second opinions, just a strong recommendation, from someone he trusts, converted into action. This is why he's a leader in his profession and an athlete on the way up.

Another athlete missed Hawaii qualification by one spot in his recent Ironman race. He sent me a text message with the roll-down results. I answered, "Enter Honu Half."

In fewer than eight hours, I received another text. "Have entered Honu Half." The next day we flew to Kona. That was action. Again, the guy runs a successful business and has a respectable portfolio of real estate investments. He acts when action is needed.

Another athlete had raced two Iron distance races, reducing his time significantly. He asked, "What next?"

I said, "Enter Port IM. I reckon you can qualify for Hawaii." In a couple of weeks, we started his Hawaii Ironman build-up. This guy went from a ninety-minute–plus swimmer to a sixty-two–minute swimmer in eighteen months. Whenever I gave him an instruction, he got it. He has the ability to turn directions into action easily. He's also prepared to do whatever it takes to improve.

Several groups of athletes I work with show enthusiasm and optimism that is exciting to be near. There's a willingness to go with something that is new to them. It's optimism that washes away any doubts or preconceived limitations. It's a no-fear attitude.

This open-ended optimism is the quality that produces great results. It's the group energy that drives the whole squad forward. People with this optimism are fast learners. They have the right mental state to turn directions into action in seconds.

I hear athletes and coaches talking about height, limb length, fast-twitch fibres, slow-twitch fibres, aerobic capacity, all sorts of equipment, GPS, HRMs, power meters, and other things they feel make a difference.

The qualities I like to see in an athlete are optimism; belief in the plan; confidence in the plan; a preparedness to do what has to be done; trust in the coach; toughness; resilience; and an ability to listen, understand, and convert directions into action.

These are the qualities I've found most successful athletes have in common. We all hear things on different wave lengths. If there's something you don't understand, speak up. If we don't quite get it, we'll never be able to convert it into action.

**After the game, the king and the
pawn go in the same box.**

When Do You Start Body Maintenance?

Do you start when something goes wrong, breaks down, or wears out? It's a far better plan to schedule regular maintenance as a preventative measure. It's not cool to be injured or getting sympathy from those close to you when you miss out on that important race.

Do you visit a physio when you become injured? The best way to use a physio's talents is before you become injured. Visit a physio to have him or her screen your body for flexibility issues and strength imbalances. A good physio can identify weaknesses long before you become injured. Simple things like upper thoracic flexibility can help you to swim faster and time trial for long distances on your bike without your neck seizing up. If you address your lack of flexibility in the upper back, you'll actually go faster in the water and then ride faster because you can hold the aero position longer.

Improving your core strength can mean that when you get off the bike with all that time you've gained by being more flexible, you can run efficiently straight out of T2. You'll be able to hold an efficient stride rhythm for the whole length of the run. Some athletes could gain half an hour in an Ironman race by doing no more training, becoming more flexible, and developing some core strength. Yet many buy a more expensive set of wheels instead.

Every training expert preaches about the importance of being consistent in training. If you don't get sick, you can keep training. You don't have to train as much each week if there are no weeks off for illness. Training a little less and keeping your immune system in great shape will produce better results through consistency.

The best time to boost your immune system is not when you get a cold. Do the things that boost your immunity before you get any symptoms of impending illness. Good nutrition is like insurance. I hear people whinge about the cost of certain supplements, saying they produce expensive urine. What does house and contents insurance produce? Big profits for the insurance company? I just paid over a thousand dollars to insure our house for a year. I don't care if I don't get to claim, and I don't care if the money goes to the shareholders of the company.

Sometimes a lot more strength and speed can be gained by doing less training and more resting, taking the right supplements, feeding/refuelling better after key sessions, and having a massage or acupuncture once a week. Every week I visit my Chinese herbalist and acupuncturist. She checks my pulse in several different positions, looks at my eyes and tongue, and asks a few questions. She then gives me whatever acupuncture or herbs she wants me to take. I don't even ask what's in them; I just boil them up and drink them. She's working with me to get the best out of this body.

As athletes get older and things don't spring back quite as quickly as before, they become more responsive to better recovery procedures. But if it helps older athletes and if professional athletes take advantage of every recovery tool available to them, why don't younger athletes get serious about maximising gains?

A few things we could all do better:

* Have 20 to 30 per cent protein in every meal. Body builders know about recovery. They're experts at it. Their sport is all about recovering muscles after breaking them down. But so is ours. We're building strong, lean muscles that can keep doing the same task over and over for a long time. While body builders are just building them to look at, the same recovery processes work.

* Have a nap after your main big session of the week. Just an hour is great to give the body a chance to recover. Look at how racehorses are treated. They're on the best diet money can buy. Just the right amount of training, a shower, a rub down, and then back in the stall to rest. They spend 80 per cent of their lives resting.

* Borrowing from the racehorse again: just the right amount of training. No serious trainer is going to flog his horse with more and more hours of training just to make his diary look good. These guys train for results. More is not better. Just the right amount is usually best.

* Different athletes have different nutritional needs. Back to the racehorses. My wife has a horse. It's an ex-racehorse, a thoroughbred. It shares a paddock with two other horses. The others just eat grass, and they stay in good condition (no ribs showing). They're all healthy and happy. Sandy's horse, Dolly, is like a big brown vacuum cleaner. She eats grass all day, and if she's not fed pellets and extra green feed every morning and night, she starts to lose weight. In fact, she's had to have coconut meal added to her feed to keep her ribs covered. She weighs 50 per cent more than the other horses do, and she eats 50 per cent more. She is beautiful, but it's a bit like having a cancer growing in your bank account.

* Balance hard days against easy days. Most of my athletes have two key sessions in a week; some have three. In-between these key sessions, we're working on technique and recovery. A lot of athletes have trained with me for one or two seasons and had great results. When they've moved on and often done more training, they've generally had worse results.

* Have a coach/trainer who can protect you from yourself. Even though I've coached hundreds of athletes to Ironman races, I have a coach for myself. Recently I did a time trial up a mountain. I was definitely stronger than the previous time I had climbed it. I got to the top, and my time was four minutes slower. When we

examined my power figures, I had gone too hard in the first half and given all my time back in the second half. I told my coach that I wanted to change my plan for the following Thursday's interval session and do the mountain again.

He talked me out of it. The interval session was forty minutes of hard stuff, whereas the mountain was one hour and twenty minutes. He said, "Stick to our plan." I knew he was right, but my ego wanted a PB. I did the interval session and recorded the best figures I have had for four years. The following Sunday, I rode a one hundred-kilometre time trial, recording the best time for a year. Sometimes we need a coach to step in between our egos and our plans. When you make a plan, there's a good reason for everything on it. Don't change it.

Attitude is the difference between an ordeal and an adventure.

Staying Well in Winter While Training to Improve

One morning I felt the first touch of winter. I'm sure my friends in southern states and in the northern hemisphere were laughing. But it's all relevant. Our Brisbane bodies are used to Brisbane temperatures. When the morning temperature drops into the low teens, our bodies struggle to cope. A percentage of our energy goes into handling the colder air going into our lungs. Just keeping warm without the load of exercise uses energy that we don't need to find in warmer weather.

Something that plants, trees, and shrubs know that many athletes don't is that in winter, when the days get shorter, it's best to do less. The trees stop growing. The lawn hardly ever needs mowing in winter. Our ancestors traditionally stored food in the summer months for the cooler part of the year when the days were shorter and food was scarce.

So, as a result of thousands of years of high activity in summer and low activity in winter, our bodies will not tolerate the same workloads in winter as they will in summer. Anyone in tune with his or her body will know that when spring comes, when the mornings get light earlier, it's easier to train. Getting out of bed is easy.

We owe it to ourselves to go with the flow, the flow of energy that is. Adjusting our workloads and our total weekly hours of training to suit the season is the first step in staying well through winter. I personally drop my training hours by 30 per cent for winter, choosing to work on specific weaknesses and technique improvement rather than volume.

The next step in staying well is the type of food we eat in colder weather. If we look at the diets of people who live in cold climates, they usually eat quite different styles of food from the warmer climates. A Russian peasant eats quite a different diet from a Thai peasant.

Our bodies will thrive on well-cooked stews, casseroles, and hearty soups in colder weather. Well cooked, juicy foods are easier to digest in cool weather than salads and raw foods are. In traditional Chinese medicine, a lot of attention is given to heat and cold in the body. Breathing cold air needs to be balanced by eating warming foods.

All of our athletes take fish-oil capsules morning and night. This helps them maintain a healthy intake of omega-3 oils that are essential in keeping immune systems in good shape. We've even found it improves cold tolerance when swimming in cold water.

Another great immune booster is vitamin C if it's taken (the way nature intended) in the company of bioflavonoids. (Blackmores bioC is a good one.) It's a good idea to boost the intake of vitamin C at the first sign of illness like a tickle or itch in the throat, excessive tiredness, restless sleep, or slight headache. Vitamin C is water soluble and is not stored in the body. It's a good idea to take it every two to three hours when under stress. Rather than suggest doses, your local health food store would have someone more qualified than me to advise.

Another item worth having in the medicine chest this time of year is a pack of zinc lozenges. Often the first signs of a dry, itchy throat can be neutralised by sucking a couple of zinc lozenges. The zinc is absorbed directly into the mouth and throat.

Another worthwhile addition to the supplement collection is a probiotic (Inner Health is a good one). The body's defence against lots of winter illness is boosted by taking a probiotic once or twice a week. Every day when you're getting close to a race or right after a tough training session, the key to a good immune system is to have the stomach in top shape.

Garlic should be included in as many meals as possible. It's often called nature's antibiotic. We use it in just about everything we cook.

Echinacea is another item worth keeping in the cupboard, along with colloidal silver. These things don't need to be taken every day, but it makes good sense to have them available for when you feel the first signs of illness.

Lots of athletes are not aware that cooling down gradually after a high heart-rate session improves the chances of avoiding illness. You should be doing it anyway to flush waste products out of the muscles. Cooling down aerobically will oxygenate the cells. Oxygen-starved cells are more susceptible to viral attack. Cool down well, and avoid getting sick.

The mind that perceives the limitation is the limitation.

Be Happy; It's the Key to Performance

How many people do you meet who are truly happy? Do you ever sit at a table in a busy shopping centre and watch people's faces as they walk by? Most of them look like they have the weight of the world on their shoulders.

Happy-looking people are becoming a rare sight. You have to be careful; wearing a frown all the time will imprint that look into your face. People's faces are a reflection of the lives they've lived. There are too many miserable people out there. This is a great country; life can be whatever you want it to be.

The happiest people I've met are not the wealthiest. They're not the fittest. They're not the most beautiful. If beauty, fitness, and wealth don't make you happy, what does?

The happiest people I've met are happy with who they are, and they're happy with what they have. It seems to be a simple formula. I've met some people who are dirt poor but love every day or their lives. I've met people whose bodies are worn out, twisted and bent, yet they look forward to every day with a smile.

It's great to have ambitions, sporting goals, and wealth-building goals. The important thing to have, immediately, is happiness with what you have. By all means, work toward having more, but contentment with what you have will make life better today. This, in turn, will make you more productive today.

How often do we see incredibly wealthy celebrities, movie stars, and sporting stars whose lives are a mess? Fame and wealth have not made them happy. They often don't like who they are. To be really happy and productive, you need to like the person you are. You can always strive to be a better person, but liking who you are today will make you feel more worthy of success.

Lots of talented athletes don't feel worthy of success. This feeling of unworthiness often shows up in silly mistakes that handicap performance— a sudden loss of motivation, a silly mistake in an important race, or letting unimportant little things get in the way of important training sessions.

There's a simple little exercise I've asked depressed people to do that has helped them turn their outlook on life around 180 degrees.

I ask them to send me an e-mail every day that lists three things:

1. Something beautiful (something they've seen that day that struck them as being beautiful).

2. Experience (something they've experienced that day that has had an impact on them—positive or negative).

3. Something nice (something nice they've done for someone else without expecting anything in return—any simple little thing).

After a week of doing this exercise every day, their eyes start to open to the world around them. After a month of being aware of the world around them, they change the way they look at our own little parts of it.

Happiness is easier to achieve than we all realise. Once we have true happiness, athletic performance comes easy. It comes from the heart.

Be strong when you are weak, be brave when you are scared, be humble when you are victorious, and be badass every day.

What Is Mental Strength?

Mental strength can take many forms. Our sport relies heavily on mental strength. In fact, it's the biggest single ingredient in an Ironman athlete's success.

Punctuality—Most of us don't realise that being punctual requires mental strength. Mental strength takes many different, often subtle, forms. To be punctual, you have to care. You have to respect the commitment you have made to the coach, to yourself. Being punctual confirms your commitment. It's often the result of sighting your goals as the alarm goes off—that moment after the alarm is shut down before you actually get up. This is where punctuality starts. Every day starts by sighting your goal, even if it's done subconsciously. It's the goal that gets you up.

Organisation—Being organised is the key to great achievement. The most common characteristic of successful Ironman athletes is the fact that they fit more into a life than normal people do. There is no incentive to become organised unless you have strong goals. People without strong goals have no need to be organised. One of the ingredients of mental strength is efficiency. You have to be organised to be efficient.

Resilience—The road to the top is never going to be one straight line without a few dips. Mentally strong athletes have the ability to take the good with the bad. They know where they're going, and they know what they want. No obstacle is going to stop them. Shit happens; get over it.

Emotions—We all have them. In fact, emotions drive us through difficult times when there's no logical reason to keep going. But we have to harness this powerful force. We have to direct our emotions toward making the right moves toward our goals. We have to be aware of our emotions and not let them distract us. Calming ourselves when things are not going right is another facet of mental strength that should not be underestimated.

Single minded—When we start a journey toward something we really want in life, it often ends up not fitting with the plans others have for us. We have to be strong if we're going to get the prize. Along the way are going to be lots of people who will stand in our paths. Some of them are going to be close friends, loved ones, employers, and even other competitors. If our goals are strong enough, we'll see a clear path through all these snags. There is always a way. It often doesn't suit others, but they just have to get used to how it is.

Masochist—The dictionary says, "A person who enjoys something that seems painful or tiring to others." Now isn't that an Ironman? If you go into this game knowing it's going to hurt and you get used to hurting in each long, tough session, you will find a feeling of satisfaction that comes from it. Learning to face some pain allows you to find the strength that lies hidden behind that pain. Then all of a sudden you start looking forward to that "pain barrier" so that you can push through and find the reward on the other side. This is one of the components of mental strength.

Ownership—You have to own your goal and defy anyone to take it from you. If you start a race already owning the spot you're chasing, you'll be a much tougher opponent than one who is trying to get his hands on the prize. Psychologically it's better to defend something you see as your own than to try to take the prize from someone else. You'll fight harder to hold your own property. This quality alone is one of the greatest assets an athlete can have.

To live is the rarest thing in the world; most people simply exist.

The Pep Talk

Confidence—It's a known fact that the single most important factor involved in achieving great results is confidence. That's not just confidence in your own ability but also in the plan to which you're working and committed. The athletes who change their programs around—add a little more here and there and take a shortcut here and there—are not confidant in the plans. They'll never get the results they seek.

Commitment—This is the driving force that gets you out of bed in the dark and gives you the power to say no to the distractions that may derail your progress. Commitment is what athletes who travel for work have when they do core-strength work in their hotel rooms and when they find a pool in a strange city to do the swim when they should. Commitment is the force that gets you organised to get everything ready the night before so that in the morning, there are no hold ups. It's also the ability to get there on time. I make sure I'm there on time. I can't expect you to be there on time if I'm not. I'm committed to giving you the best coaching possible. Are you committed to being the best athlete you can be?

Details— While I am more focussed on the big picture, some details are very important. I'm not a nitpicker. I really don't care if a one hundred-kilometre ride turns out to be ninety-eight kilometres. I am not worried if you can save seventeen seconds over forty kilometres with an aero helmet or if the Hed Jet wheel is any lighter than the Hed Alp. But I do care if you don't hold your belly in when you do your leg extensions. And I do care if you do your aerobic run intervals fifteen seconds faster than I have specified. And how well you refuel yourself after training is really important to me.

Excellence—This is the difference between contenders and pretenders. Excellence equals confidence. Confidence equals results. If you have read the many books and stories about the great Mark Allen, you'll realise he had all of the bases covered. No one was more committed. He accepted nothing less than excellence from himself or those around him. His attention to detail was legendary, and all this converted to an unshakable confidence on race day. You may say he was a professional athlete with nothing else in his life to worry about. If you can excuse it away as easy as that, then it leads us to the next factor involved in producing great results.

Excuses—We all have them. To achieve our individual potential, we have to become very good at identifying excuses as soon as they appear. Excuses are very sneaky little things. They disguise themselves as reasons. They are really reasons to fail. They'll try to convince you that they're really looking after your lifestyle. Maybe protecting you from becoming obsessed. Whenever you feel an excuse trying to sneak into your world, an excuse that may alter your path, remember that the view from the podium is always much better than the view from the audience.

Behind every successful person is a substantial amount of coffee.

Building Your Self-Image

It's unusual for a teenager to have a well-developed self-image. There are exceptions. Often these kids are the sports champions who have grown up being good at something. Every win builds their confidence, and they expect to win, which makes it more likely that next time they race they will win.

Many of us have come into triathlon without any real success in any of the sports involved. And many of us have had rather humbling experiences in our first few attempts.

Most of us really don't know how others see us. We often imagine that others actually care what our results are. Who are we kidding? Triathletes are the most self-centred bunch of people you'll ever meet. Don't get me wrong here, some of the finest people I have ever met are triathletes. But ask them what time you did in your last race, and they'll look blank. They really are mainly interested in their own results and training progress.

One of the biggest mistakes you can make is to measure yourself against your training partners. Use your own time trials and race results to measure your progress.

To race faster, you have to build your expectations along with your fitness, technique, and strength. Building strength and fitness and improving technique is all just a matter of time spent following a sensible program, following a good diet, and practicing perfection. In order to build your expectations, you need to develop a strong self-image. You really have to like who you are.

To build that strong positive self-image, you need to be nice to yourself. You need to compliment yourself when you achieve something, such as climbing a hill in a higher gear, swimming a PB in the pool, or a faster race result.

All of these examples are of you beating yourself. This is the only real measure of progress. If you pin your progress on someone else's performances, you'll set yourself up for disappointment. Other athletes may improve at a different rate from you. You may be a steady, long-term improver, while your training mate might be going through a stage of rapid improvement only to slow down in the future. Also, there's the chance your training mate has so much untapped talent that he'll be a future champion of the sport.

There's also the real chance that your training mate is a perfectionist, someone dedicated to doing everything right—dotting every *i* and crossing every *t*. Many of our Hawaii Ironman winners have proved that this approach pays off. Doing everything right and sticking at it for a long time has a scary way of uncovering talent you didn't even know existed.

Keeping a diary is a great way to build self-image. I suggest you only record the wins. When I look at your diary, I don't want to see what went wrong; I want to see what went right. When you look back over that diary and see all the good things, you're able to see your progress in black and white. You may think you'll remember it, but if you write it down, it's there. Also, the actual act of writing it down imprints it into your subconscious mind as a permanent record.

Self-image, whether it's strong or weak, is recorded in your subconscious mind. It's part of who you are. It can only be changed a little at a time. You can't hear Anthony Robbins speak and instantly become a winner.

Becoming a winner is a step-by-step process. Lots of small wins add up to you seeing yourself as a winner.

**What you tell yourself every day will
either lift you up or tear you down.**

Do You Think You're a Bit Too Fat to Be Fast?

Why is it that girls who have visible six-packs ask me if I think they could drop a couple of kilos.

I can't remember how many times I've told them to train for health and good recovery. The weight will automatically become what is ideal for them.

It seems that this idea that they're fat is more prevalent after a major race. Maybe something hormonal switches on after they lighten their training load. Maybe they have too much time on their hands.

We can't train at the same volume all year; we'd just burn out. Maybe we need to find something else to fill our time while we let the body catch up.

Another thing likely to "do the heads in" on the girls is weighing themselves too often. I'd rather see our girls never weigh themselves. As we train and develop the athlete, fat levels drop, and muscle density increases.

A girl can be looking fabulous, but the scales will suggest she hasn't lost any weight, or worse still, she may have gained weight.

I would much rather the girls and guys in the squad use the belly-button test. Lie on your back, put your finger tip into your belly button, squeeze the skin between the fore finger and thumb. If it's thicker than one centimetre, we'll train until it is one centimetre. If it is one centimetre, it's just right for an endurance athlete.

It doesn't matter what you weigh. Scales only tell you figures. They have very little to do with going faster.

Eating for good health is what will make you go faster and keep you looking good for a long time into the future.

As we grow up, we realise it's less important to have lots of friend and more important to have real ones.

Toughness

Without doubt, toughness is one of the greatest assets an Ironman triathlete can hold.

But I have known guys who were so tough a cat couldn't scratch them, and they only ever put in mediocre Ironman races. Because they were dumb. They were uncoachable. If they were working dogs on a rural property, their owners would have shot them. Toughness without self-control is as useful as an ashtray on a motorcycle.

Toughness alone is not the key. I have two friends who are ex-SAS soldiers. Both retired as officers after spending years training the best of the best. Both of my friends have raced Ironman.

These two guys have both told me that in the SAS, what they searched for was a balance between toughness, patience, coolness, and the ability to think things through before acting.

In his book, *The Coach*, Rick Charlesworth, the coach of Australia's women's hockey team to three-consecutive Olympic Gold medals, describes his definition of mental strength as resilience, the ability spring back from shock, depression or upset, and keep going.

I'm looking for the following in my ideal Ironman athlete:

1. The toughness to "guts it out" when conditions are at their worst in training and racing, without even thinking of complaining. Some athletes actually enjoy being tested in the very worst conditions. They look forward to being tested.

2. The intelligence to instinctively know when it's time to modify the plan. A slight change in plan may save a race or even save a life.

3. The courage to step out into the unknown, to give it a go, and to face fear and overrule it. The courage to work toward a goal that everybody around you tells you is out of your league. The courage to hold back in training instead of racing the others so that there is more in the bank on race day.

4. The commitment to do all of the little things right like the core-strength work, stretching, refuelling, alternative therapies, equipment maintenance, visualisation, resting, and balancing life with other interests.

5. The toughness to dredge the bottom of the barrel in the last twenty kilometres of the run, when the results are truly decided. The ability to overrule all of the body's cries for relief.

I've got a dream that's worth more than my sleep.

Self-Doubt

I remember sitting in the audience in Kona one year when Paula Newby-Fraser made her acceptance speech, surprised to hear that she had to give herself a "talking to" halfway through the Hawaii Ironman run. She was leading at the time.

She told the audience she stopped and thought she could not go on. She was leading by a good margin. She said to herself, "Paula, pull yourself together; you can do it." She went on to win.

Paula has the greatest number of victories in the Hawaii Ironman. If Paula has patches of self-doubt, accept that it's normal to sometimes doubt yourself during a race and in the weeks leading into a major race.

I have coached athletes of all levels. It may surprise some that the athletes most likely to speak to their coach about self-doubt are the most talented. I think there are two reasons for this.

First, the most talented athletes develop a close partnership with their coaches and are more likely to discuss these things.

Second, high achievers have high expectations. High expectations can put greater pressure on athletes to perform. Not only their own expectations but also the expectations of others can cause them to sometimes doubt their abilities.

If the self-doubt monster creeps into your mind, be ready; expect him. The enemy who surprises you has an instant advantage. If you're expecting the enemy, you're ready. It's like an ambush. Have your ammunition ready.

The ammunition you need to beat self-doubt is evidence of your readiness. Evidence of the thorough preparation you've done. Evidence of your ability and your strengths. Think of what your coach says that snaps you out of self-doubt. It's all of the above.

You may not have access to your coach at that moment of need, but if you have been keeping a diary and recording all the achievements, all the wins in training, and only what went right, that's what you'll find when you look back through it.

It's a mistake to record what went wrong. We don't need to be reminded of the negatives. Recording all the positives imprints the message into our subconscious minds. Lots of little reinforcements add up to a strong core of self-belief.

I prefer a diary written by hand, on paper the old fashioned way. It's real. It's accessible whether you're in a strange country, in an airport lounge, or on a flight. You can be sitting on a beach, alone, the day before a major event. You can flick through the pages of your diary and relive a few of the wins you've experienced.

Every time you have a win, search for an affirmation that can connect you with that moment in time. Often using that affirmation in a race can keep you in a winning state of mind.

I've been talking about wins. Many of us will never win a race, but as triathletes, we have wins every day we train. It's not just about coming across the line first. Often it's about doing something a little better than ever before. Maybe going a fraction of a second faster than ever before in a time trial. It might even be completing everything on our programs for a whole month.

All of these simple things can add to your core of self-belief. These simple things can be used to combat self-doubt, if you have enough of them.

Surround yourself with the dreamers and the doers, the believers and the thinkers. Most of all, surround yourself with those who see the greatness within you, even when you don't see it yourself.

Do You Want the Merc Before You Do the Work?

I've recently been involved in a conversation about coaching the Generation Y athletes. These are the "young guns" who have grown up getting things without having to work too hard for them.

They're a major worry for coaches around the country. It has been suggested that traditional coaching approaches don't work on this group. The coaching staff of large football teams, of all codes, are faced with the problem of building teams that will work together, for the common good, with Gen Y kids.

I'm fortunate to be involved in training adults. This is less of a problem with adults, but some have been influenced by the age of instant gratification.

It seems that in an age where our parents cater to our every need, entertainment, transport, positive reinforcement, money, and protection, we are producing soft kids. Is it any wonder why the best juniors in the triathlon world are coming from Mexico, Argentina, and Eastern Europe?

This problem is not limited to the kids. I know adults who have grown up with mothers who were too sympathetic. Most of the sooks I've known were created by sympathetic mothers or wives.

The Gen Y group need to be entertained all the time. They have short attention spans. They are prepared to do the work if it's fun and interesting. If it's mundane, foundation-laying stuff, you'll lose them. I recently let a talented young guy slip through my net because he was just not going to make it. He had grandiose plans of what he wanted, but when it came time to lay the solid foundations for such plans, he was not on the same page. I'm not going to change pages for some young guy whose mum has spent the past eighteen years packing him in cotton wool and making excuses for him. I could entertain him over the next few years, catering for his "special needs." But one important day I won't be there, and his mum won't be there. He'll discover the world can be a cruel, hard place for a mummy's boy.

We've been attracted to this sport because we want to be tested. We want to know how we perform when the chips are down. Whether we're aware of this or not, it's this part of the sport that attracts most of us.

To do well, we have to be prepared. To be prepared, we have to do lots of steady, base-building stuff. This is not racing a bunch of pretenders around a city circuit for an hour or so and finishing it off with a cappuccino. This may be interesting and exciting, and you may get to dress up like a real cyclist. But to perform in a real race, at a level you have never reached before, is going to take lots of hours of less interesting, less exciting, and almost boring training.

Training for an Ironman has many parallels with business. We all know people in business who go straight for the trappings of wealth before they have accumulated the wealth. The big house, the pool, the luxury cars, and every electrical gadget known to man. As soon as there's a downturn in business, the panic sets in. Instead of building a business (laying a foundation) and then letting it provide the trappings of wealth, we see these people squeezing the life out of the business to pay for the image of wealth (trying to support a lifestyle on little, if any, foundation).

Like in business, laying foundations is not that exciting. It's mundane, repetitive work that just has to be done. When the right foundations have been laid, the rewards start to flow back in ever increasing waves.

Again, like in business, you have to dedicate time each season to work on your foundations. Always adding and always strengthening the base. If you're good at something, maintain it, and add some value to something you're not as good at.

The most successful people I've ever met are hard workers. They may be incredibly successful, and they keep working at it. They're good at time management and always have time for what's important. Great innovators are always looking for an improvement. They handle setbacks in stride. It's like they expect some setbacks; they just pause for a moment and find another way to get the job done. They have long-term plans and are not seeking instant gratification. They're prepared to do the work and then buy the Merc.

You were born with the ability to change someone's life; don't ever waste it.

Do You Just Feel Like Crying?

When you're training hard, it's tough to fit everything in: enough sleep, cooking healthy meals, getting everything ready for the next day, and cleaning up. You're pushed to your limits at each moment. Right when you think you're going flat out, you might find a little bit more pressure is added.

If you crack, have a little cry, lose direction for a moment, snarl at someone close, and then don't worry about it. It's normal.

When you run across that line, and Mike Riley calls, "You're an Ironman," he doesn't just mean you've swum 3.8 kilometres, cycled 180 kilometres, and run 42 kilometres; he means you've done the whole journey—the early mornings and the three attempts to get out of bed to train. He means you have survived the six months to get here and then done one big day to finish it all off.

I've often told athletes in the squad the Ironman is not a one-day event. It's a six-month event, finishing with one big day.

No matter which race you're doing, whether you're a talented pro or a first-time Ironman competitor, I'd be pushing you close to the edge.

I'd be watching feedback, whether it's by e-mail or visual. The feedback helps me to know how close to the edge you are.

I can tell when I read e-mails from online athletes if they were smiling when they wrote them. There's something in a person's choice of words that gives it away. Sometimes it's the way that communication slows down or stops, which gives me a clue.

The athletes in the squad who I get to see regularly can't hide their body language. Sometimes it's the way they walk; sometimes it's the way they look when I read out the workout.

One of the symptoms of being tired is self-doubt. Don't feel like you're the only one feeling it. The most talented athletes in the world have moments of self-doubt. When you get this feeling, welcome it. It's an opportunity, an opportunity to overcome it.

On race day, you're going to be tired at some time. Most likely you're going to be very tired. When you're very tired you'll feel self-doubt creep into your mind. You'll hear your "weak you" speaking in your ear, telling you its too hard and that you can't keep the pace up. You can't go on.

Are you going to listen? Did you listen in training? Did you beat self-doubt when it tried to get you to sleep in? Didn't you beat self-doubt when it said you couldn't make that time base? Did self-doubt tell you that you shouldn't train three days out from a less important race?

If self-doubt caused you to make decisions in training, then you have given self-doubt the strength to control your life.

Every time your weak you or self-doubt challenges you and you win by overruling the doubts, you become stronger, and self-doubt becomes weaker.

Winning makes you stronger; it becomes a habit.

The major battle you face on race day is not against your competitors or the course. The battle is with your own mind.

Right now is when you lay the foundations for winning that battle on race day. Right now is when you lay the foundations for winning that battle on race day. Races are not won early in the day. The Ironman is won late in the day, when the mind is tired. The body is exhausted. That little voice inside your head is starting to talk you down. That's when the habit of making the right decisions is the most valuable tool at your disposal.

Many of the workouts at this time of the preparation are designed to be 70 per cent for the mind and 30 per cent for the body. If you can find a good reason to not complete one, you'll very likely find a reason on race day to take your foot off the accelerator.

Every Sunday morning when the alarm goes off, don't get up to improve your cycling or your running. Anyone can do that. Get up to go out and build the inner athlete, an athlete with a mental strength so tough, so resilient, that nothing can stand in the way of getting what you want.

So, if you feel like crying, the greatest athletes have felt just like that. If the voice inside your head says you can't keep going, the toughest athletes in the world have felt like that.

One very important thing to never forget: the greatest athletes in the world are people just like you. They have all the same doubts and fears. They are just more skilled at handling them.

Here's to the people who love us, the losers who lost us, and the lucky bastards who get to meet us.

Discipline—Who Needs It?

We often hate to be told what to do. We want to chart our own paths in life. Anyone who has raised teenagers knows how they resist direction, even though they know it's in their best interests.

I've found young guys might rebel against discipline. But once they realise there are definite boundaries, they settle down and actually feel more comfortable focusing on their chosen directions.

I have to have a coach to keep me answerable so that I get in and swim when the weather is less than perfect and do the hard intervals on the wind trainer. I actually enjoy having someone to push me. There is something inside every one of us that makes us want to please the teacher, our parents, or our coaches. I guess I'm looking for some positive feedback. Even in my sixties, I'm still trying to please my coach.

I pay my coach more than I charge my athletes because he gives me more of a personal service. He has fewer athletes under his direction.

One of the main benefits I receive from my coach is discipline. He's always checking my swim technique. I may feel like a winner, but he tells me when I don't look like one. I trust his judgement. We have worked together for about three years and have gotten to know each other well. He knows what I need, and I know what he expects.

Each season he gives me four "get out of jail cards" to be used in those times when I just don't have the energy to train and need to cancel. Each season I get to the end with at least one card left. That's the discipline he brings to the relationship.

It doesn't matter if you're a raw beginner or an experienced pro, you'll gain more if you have someone to answer to who has your best interests at heart. Someone who holds you back when you need it and pushes you forward when you need it. Someone who pats your back or kicks your a*se when you need it.

Athletes who resist that discipline simply are not committed to the goals they have chosen. If your ego stands in the way of your progress, you'll never reach your potential.

The greatest heroes in history have all been incredibly disciplined. There are so many examples of great leaders who have been so disciplined personally that they inspired those who followed them, by their own examples.

One of the greatest stories I have read of discipline and leadership is that of Earnest Shackleton's Antarctic expedition. In 1914 the expedition was lost for two years, and every man survived because of the leadership and the discipline of the whole crew. Their ship was crushed by the pack ice, and they were left to drift on the ice pack. This was in the days before radios, GPS, and all of our modern navigational aids.

In fact, discipline can be a very empowering experience. Our sport seems to attract people who thrive on discipline. If we can identify that quality in us that is strengthened by discipline and use the strengthening effect to build our confidence, we can tap into this great tool to benefit race performance.

Discipline is like a muscle. Every time it's exercised, it becomes a little stronger. It's actually your mental strength that you're exercising.

I love the smell of success in the morning.

Your Self-Talk Shapes the Life You Will Live

Be careful what you think or say to yourself. Not only does your self-talk influence your body language, it also shapes the life you will live. I have a few examples I'd like to share.

I was sitting with an athlete watching her husband finish his workout one Sunday morning. She said, "I wish I could run like X; he makes it look easy. He actually looks like he's enjoying it." I told her that for him, it is easy. When I see her running, it's like she's saying to herself, "This is bullshit." She burst out laughing because that's exactly what she was thinking to herself. I could read it in her body language. We've since modified her self-talk, and last Sunday I rode up behind her when she was running after a tough bike ride. Her body language has totally changed, and she is now a runner. She actually enjoys it now, as it's becoming easy for her.

Recently I had lunch with a good mate who has trained with us in the past. He trains with a few different groups these days, mainly socially. I encouraged him to join us one morning for an early morning bike ride up and over the mountain. He said he'd like to. He said he'd try to make it. If you'd like to do something, or if you try to make it, it's not the same as being there—making a commitment and turning up. After our discussion, he was there that morning in the dark. He enjoyed the ride and the banter over coffee afterward. Remember, there is no *try*; there's *do* or *do not*. You don't become world champion by trying to be world champion.

One Sunday I had quite a few athletes racing in the Cairns Ironman. I'd been talking to each of them regarding the mental attitude they were to take into the race. It's so important to be totally committed to a course of action. Especially when the race you're about to do is going to thoroughly test your resolve. You have to know what you're there for, and you have to know how you're going to handle the test. One of the athletes had said, "I'm going to smash it; I have nothing to lose."

I agree he had nothing to lose, but the affirmation could very well have caused him to actually lose all he'd worked for. The words in the affirmation were far from ideal. Our subconscious minds read words as positive or negative. The words *nothing* and *lose* are both negative. Changing them to "I have everything to gain" is a much more powerful affirmation. The fact that it starts with "I" turns on our subconscious. *Everything* and *gain* are winners words. If you have access to a kinesiologist, ask him to muscle test you with these two affirmations. You'll soon choose the one you'll use in your next race.

Next time you ride into a headwind or ride up a steep hill, use the affirmation, "This is a great life" or "I am so lucky to be able to do this." The wind does not seem so strong, and the hill does not seem so steep. The power of the mind is amazing. I could have said, "The power of the mind is unbelievable." But *amazing* is a much more powerful word than *unbelievable*. We should set out to live an amazing life, because living an amazing life is totally believable. Anyone who does an Ironman triathlon is living an amazing life.

Another of my athletes told me he was a little sore and sniffly four days before race day. He said he was hoping to be feeling better as the week went by. Hoping is not the best way to get what you want. We use these words without really thinking. I've heard that hope is disappointment postponed. Be aware that by using the words *try, hope,* and *wish,* you're not exactly constructing the life you want. It's painting a mental picture of what would be nice if it came into being, but it's not setting a plan of action for attaining these things.

The athlete hoping to feel better is a seasoned competitor. In one of his most successful races, I asked him to give me 570 efficient minutes in his race. Just focus on producing efficient minutes. After he was finished, we looked at his time. He had taken 571 minutes to complete the race. He didn't do that race hoping to do well. He simply did what he had to do in order to achieve the goal. Action will always out-produce hope. If he spends this week eating well and resting well, he'll still be "the man" on race day.

It may be pleasant sitting by the pool in the warm winter sunshine, hoping to swim faster next season. Taking action often ensures that you will swim faster next season. A couple of the athletes in the squad are great examples, they're very good at being consistent in training. Their personality types have them focused on doing every little thing well. These athletes race well. They live a life of action. They're willing workers doing everything I ask of them. They don't find reasons why they should miss something. Their self-talk is simply, "Do the job." Don't question it; lay each brick in the wall. When they race, they don't have to think too much; they do the job really well. Their job is to produce efficient minutes.

A large number of this generation are total pussies, whose primary focus is finding things to be offended by. (I have included a couple of affirmations specifically for them.)

Racing with Your Mind and Your Stomach

Anyone who has raced an Ironman well will agree it's done with the mind.

That's true. But no matter how mentally prepared you might be, if the fuel is not getting through to the legs, it's not going to be as good as it could be.

So we're about to set out on a mission where we have to have a stomach in top working order. Not a sack into which we toss whatever the hot box has sitting in it ready to go. Save all the fast-food options for after the race.

Start preparing your stomach two weeks before race day. A stressed stomach will not be back to top operating order in under a week. Pre-race nerves will very likely have an effect in the last two or three days before race day, so start now to get it right.

* Cut out coffee during your two-week taper. If you must have it, don't have it with meals and only one per day. Remember that caffeine is an easy drug to wean yourself off, and you'll get a much greater boost from it when you take your first Coke on race day if your system is clean.

* Don't eat deep-fried foods. That's simple enough. Just don't do it. They're too difficult to digest. Give your stomach a break. Fried is okay if it's you frying some

fish in a little fresh olive oil. But I'll guarantee the local fish shop oil has been used lots before you came along, making it almost impossible to digest.

*   Eat live foods. If they go rotten in a few days, it's usually a good sign that they have all the natural enzymes in them to help them break down. We need those enzymes to help us digest them. Most of the over-processed crap you buy from a supermarket has the natural enzymes destroyed or powerful preservatives added to stop them working. Those preservatives are not going to help your stomach be in top working order on race day.

*   Eat 60 per cent vegetables. You need to carbo load. Do it with vegetables and rice as much as possible. Wheat products are often hard to digest and slow to move through your system. A diet with lots of fish, rice, and vegetables will be easy to digest and be kind to your stomach. Your stomach will reward you on race day by doing what it can to help you get that PB.

*   Learn to relax. A high percentage of stomach issues are related to stress. A glass of wine fifteen minutes before your dinner will help you to relax and improve digestion. I did say "a glass." Just lay off the alcohol in the last three days, as any alcohol affects the liver's ability to store glycogen and will affect your ability to handle heat. There are a lot of long-term health benefits to be gained from a glass of wine at the end of the day.

* Don't eat too close to bedtime. A short walk after dinner is going to be good for your stomach and your relationship.

* Don't eat dessert. We all like sweet things now and then. Sweets eaten (even fruit) after a meal containing protein (and every meal should contain protein) will sit in the stomach fermenting, as the protein is processed slowly ahead of it. Burping and farting are not cool. We're not in high school now.

* Learn to meditate. The total body relaxation gained from meditation is going to be good for your stomach and your mind.

* On race day, don't try to overfeed. Most stomach issues in races are caused by trying to digest too much. The average stomach can only absorb a 6-per cent solution of carbs. If you take a gel, you must wash it down with water, not sports drink. Make sure your sports drinks are mixed to a 6-per cent dilution rate. If you overload your stomach with excess carbs, it'll shut down and stop absorbing everything, including water.

Use your last few long workouts as a guide. On race day, are you going to try to absorb more than you did in your last long workout? Why? Do you fear running out of fuel? Did you run out of fuel when you did that last long workout? Did you have pre-workout nerves interfering with your absorption?

If your stomach can't absorb it, you can't use it for muscle fuel.

Your mind is stronger than your legs. Giving your legs the best fuel supply will allow you to drive them harder on race day.

When an illness is part of your spiritual journey, no medical intervention can heal you until your spirit has begun to make the changes that the illness was meant to inspire.

How Important Is Failure in Building a Mentally Tough Athlete?

Have you ever met anyone who has never experienced failure? If you have, he was probably a spoilt little boy who has been sheltered from life's knocks. He'll probably need propping up all through his life.

When my son didn't make it into the first eight in his high school rowing team, my wife was devastated. She was so sad for him. It was his goal since he started rowing. Mothers feel the pain of their offspring as though it were their own pain.

I was happy for him. Of course his mother thought that was terrible. I was happy for him because he had not fully committed to the goal. He thought he had, but I could see gaps in his commitment all over the place. He was always in contention for the top eight. He was so close, and he had the talent, but others wanted it more.

If he had gotten into the top team without doing everything in his power to make it, he would have walked away thinking he could get to the top in life without giving everything.

After much soul searching, he now realises he could have made it. After all the dust has settled, it is only a high school rowing team. If he walks away from the experience having learnt a valuable lesson, he's won. High school is for learning. Winning is good, but learning is better.

My approach of welcoming failure in an athlete's development is not always popular. But in the end, I'm not doing this for popularity. I am as driven for coaching success as any of my athletes are for winning.

Some of the best performances I've assisted athletes to have come in the next big race after a shocker.

If you were disappointed with your last race, how you handle that disappointment will shape your life from here on. The toughest competitors will derive a greater level of motivation and a stronger drive to get it right next time. Mental toughness is not just about outsuffering the opposition. True mental toughness is more about how you handle things that don't go right.

Welcome failure. Failure is a report card. It just tells you where you are right now. If you're not happy with the report card, do something about it. By changing the way you view failure, you can change the future.

The best friend failure has is truth. Truthfully examining the reasons for failure can be the secret to improvement. Don't "piss in your own pocket" when examining why the failure to perform actually happened.

If your reasons for failing to reach your goal are things like lack of talent, not being tall enough, bad luck, and so on, you're kidding yourself. I'm sure an athlete with your talent level and your height could make better luck happen on the day by training and preparing better, by wanting it more, and by fighting harder to get it.

When I stood on the stage at the presentations at Busselton, West Australia, in 2006, I was in third place. The Swiss/German guy, who came first, shook hands and said in a perfect Colonel Klink accent, "So, I caught you, heh?" He had beaten me fair and square. I had stuffed up a good race. I was fit, had trained well, and was experienced. I had already done thirty IM races. I had run twenty IM marathons, twenty minutes faster.

To this day, that voice motivates me. "So, I caught you, heh?" I am doing something about it.

We don't meet people by accident; they are meet to cross our paths for a reason.

If There's a Secret, It's Confidence

Over the years, I've met lots of talented athletes. Many have achieved their goals, but sadly, many have not. The difference between the successful ones and the unsuccessful ones is not ability.

One athlete I have privately identified as the most talented athlete I've ever known didn't make it. He's still around the sport on the fringes but not competing. This guy was so technically superior and physiologically gifted he could have done anything he'd wished in our sport.

The missing ingredient was self-belief. I felt, at the time, as though I'd failed in my job. Other athletes who displayed less natural ability were able to be moulded. Their self-belief was able to be built to levels where they aimed higher than they'd ever dreamed possible and then backed up those dreams with results.

Every workout on our training program is designed to build confidence as well as strength and fitness. Often the self-coached athlete focuses on the strength and fitness sides of training while ignoring the confidence-building angles.

It's amazing how individuals can be subtly influenced by newsletter articles, brief conversations, group activities, and reading inspirational material. While others may read all the right books, have the same coaches, and do all the same workouts but never really believe in themselves enough to lay it on the line.

Over the years, my daughter, Phoebe, has listened to conversations I've had with athletes and other family members and has absorbed the message along the way. Recently, she drew my attention to something she'd read in a book: I never seek to defeat the man I am fighting; I seek to defeat his confidence. A mind troubled by doubt cannot focus on the course to victory. Two men are equals, only when they have equal confidence.

Never regret a day in your life. Good days give happiness, bad days give experience, worse days give lessons, and the best days give memories.

After All the Work Is Done—Emotions Can Make or Break the Day

We all know how being around some people drags you down. There are some people I will not spend time with. It's not my job to lift them up. In fact, the chronically negative people actually don't want to be lifted. Some people actually drain your energy. In the Harry Potter movies there were characters called "Dementors." They'd suck the joy and energy out of other characters. These are not the type of people to share with when you travel away to a race.

By the time you stand at the start line, we have built your confidence and self-belief to a level higher than ever before, by simply following the program and completing the series of confidence-building experiences. Training and suffering along with your motivated mates has bonded you together as a team. This confidence is a weapon; guard it carefully. During a three- or four-month Ironman build-up period, a real affection develops between team members. This is a powerful force.

Getting the best out of a team or an individual is not just about lots of training. These athletes are living, breathing people, who feel things. Their emotions can change in a millisecond. In fact, we are feeling things every second of the day, and our goals and dreams influence these feelings as often as our doubts and fears interfere with them. It's a constant balancing act. The most successful long-course athletes are good at taking in all the information, feelings, and thoughts and sorting them into their right boxes quickly.

This is not a skill we can master in one weekend or on one training ride. It's a way of living. Every day you have the opportunity to react to every ripple in the pond or let the ripple flow over you. This is going to happen in your long races; there are going to be ripples. Are they going to affect you? How you live your life is going to be how you handle yourself on race day.

Accept that we all have emotions. We all feel fear, affection, despair, love, anger, aggression, and many more. Accept that we have a job to do. Selecting the emotion that empowers us most, holding it, and linking it to an affirmation will give us the best results. Explore the emotion and the appropriate affirmation in training to see which one keeps you on target best. When you find the right combination, the time will go by fast. The wind will not seem so bad, and the sun will not seem so hot. You'll know when you have it.

Using the affirmation that turns on the most powerful emotion will jack up your power output in bike intervals by as much as thirty to forty watts. This is power for nothing. This works by using the right affirmation and the right emotion to neutralise the hand brakes, which the negative emotions apply to your performance.

It's really about you, being the best athlete you can be. No one else is involved in this process; it's all happening inside you. Not just in your head, emotions are all-body feelings. Learning how to handle these things can change not only your race outcomes but also your life and your interactions with others. The shortcut to finding this process is living in the moment—no thoughts about the future, no thoughts about the past.

Intelligent people tend to have fewer friends than the average person does. The smarter you are, the more selective you become.

Do We Overthink Getting out of Bed for a Training Session?

As the coach, I have high expectations. I also lead by example, I can't expect athletes to be on time, if I arrive a few minutes late. So I make sure I am always early. Before I go to bed in the evening I place my cycling gear out so when my alarm goes off, I'm out of bed and dressed in less than five minutes. It annoys my wife, but it's my discipline, I have to stick to it. I know exactly what time I have to leave home to arrive at the pool early. In twenty five years I have only arrived late twice.

Too many of us spend a little too much time thinking when that alarm goes off. Too many of us have an alternative that we consider before we get up and do what we'd planned. Getting up as soon as the alarm goes off has to become a habit. Staying in and going back to sleep can soon become a habit. Successful lives are shaped by habits. Those habits are reinforced by regular routines.

Ask any mother of young children how important routines are. Humans are very like animals the way they respond to routines. When we train our dogs or horses, they quickly learn the routines they must follow to enjoy the rewards. My dogs know by what clothes we wear as we come down the steps whether they're going running or not. If I open the cupboard door where we keep the leads, they're around at the side gate ready to go. As soon as they hear the cupboard door, they switch on to the "going for a walk" routine. I always go the same route, and when we get to the coffee shop, they know where to sit.

I always feed them after everyone else in "the pack" has eaten. From this they learn that they're at the bottom of the pecking order. Our little blue heeler, Mali, knows that she doesn't get her food until she gives me a high five. She sits and starts high-fiving as soon as I walk out the back door with her feed. The routine leads to reward. Sandy's horse, Dolly, has learned that when she goes into the float, there's some hay waiting for her. Once she's done her training and the saddle comes off, she's looking into her feed bin. Work equals reward.

As humans, we're smart enough to set up our own reward-based routines. If we can identify the reward we get after a session, starting that session is easy. Following our routines is easy because it ends in reward. The reward for joining mates in an early morning ride or run might be sharing a laugh and a coffee. It can be the feeling of satisfaction we get from sticking to the plan. Just the simple feeling training gives is enough to trigger the routine. If that routine is the same every day, it becomes a healthy habit.

Our success as athletes relies on the habits we develop— the standard routines we follow each day. Training an endurance athlete is 80 per cent routine work. Slight variations on a basic plan, adjusted to suit how close we are to an event and how well we've recovered from the previous session. A basic template can work week in, week out. Consistency is a major influence on outcomes. The people who stick to a routine every day and every week, gradually move ahead of the athletes who are always looking for something new.

If we can identify what reward we receive for being tough in training or racing, it's going to be easier to turn it on. Many of us enjoy the respect of our friends and fellow athletes when we really tough out a hard workout. It takes courage to stick at something when your whole body is screaming at you to stop. Turning on that courage to complete anything your coach gives you will earn respect both from the coach and your fellow squad members. So there's a simple formula: courage earns respect. Apply that courage whenever things get tough, and it becomes a habit, a winning habit. It's just what you do.

When the alarm goes off, don't think; do it.

A person who can read and doesn't is no better than one who cannot read.

The Power Within

I've always told the guys in the squad to look after one square metre and one minute at a time. It's such a hard skill to learn. When I go to work on Monday, after racing on the weekend, the guys at work ask, "Did you win?" I offer a lengthy, painful explanation about how age-group triathlon is not so much about winning as it is improving times, being healthy, and staying fit. They just don't get it.

When your football team plays, all you think about is winning. That's all the journalists talk about—how many wins and how many losses a team has had in the season. The worst thing the players can do is go out thinking about the end result. Football coaches emphasize the importance of sticking to the plan, working the basics, and sticking to the set plays. It's the basic, no-frills type of football that puts the flamboyant stars into positions from where they can work their magic.

It's a lot like that in the longer triathlons. When you're halfway through a long and boring bike leg, in strong winds and grinding your way home, it really doesn't matter if you have the latest GPS or the latest drinking system fitted to your bike. It comes down to basic toughness and confidence in your own ability to apply pressure to those pedals evenly, over and over and over again, without ever losing sight of the job at hand. Never waste energy thinking about the final outcome; just get the basics right.

The ability to concentrate on the job seems to be the most valuable skill an athlete can develop. But how many athletes do training directly aimed at developing this skill? We all spend hundreds of hours training our bodies to develop the skills involved in swimming. The catch, the push, the recovery, and the entry—we can do them in our sleep. But when a coach asks the squad to swim a two thousand-metre continuous effort, the moans that come from the squad would make you think they'd been asked to do something hard. For a lot of those athletes, concentrating for thirty or forty minutes is the hardest thing they could imagine. What's going to happen when they have to swim 3.8 kilometres in a race?

I have noticed the same weakness show up when I suggest that we do a 120-kilometre bike time trial. All of a sudden the squad is reduced to the "hard men." A whole lot of excuses and reasons show up why some people can't be there. Coaches don't put these things into training programs to punish people. We're not into punishing; we're into identifying weaknesses and correcting them. Learning to concentrate is correcting one of the most common weaknesses in triathlon. Long time trials are great for this.

It's funny, but the type of training you like the least is usually the type of stuff you need most. To move ahead and to get what you want out of this sport, you have to trust your coach. Keep in mind, if you're successful, you make him or her look good. You should both be working in the same direction. The moment you start to doubt whether or not you're on the right path, you're lost. It's over.

The same thing happens in really tough conditions. As soon as you "lose it," that's the belief that you can be successful. Unless you can "get it back," it's game over. Losing focus is not something limited to a few age-group triathletes. People in all walks of life do it all the time. Giving up on something when you're halfway there is so common. It's almost an epidemic.

The most important asset the successful athletes have is the ability to "get it back when they lose it." The guys and girls who we all see out at the front of the field and the ones standing on the podium at the presentations are humans just like you and me. They have times when they doubt themselves. Of course they do. They've developed the ability to get it back in seconds. They may lose it many times in a long, hard race, but they have a strategy in place to recognise what's happening, and they're able to switch it back on. That's the skill that each of us needs to develop in order to race to our potential.

The first step is recognition of what's happening. Be aware of self-doubt; it sneaks up on you.

The next step is change what you're doing. Often going harder is a perfect antidote to self-doubt. What have you got to lose? If you keep ploughing along convinced that it's just not your day, you're going to have a bad result anyway. Why not go out in a blaze of glory. Just say to yourself, "This is crap. This isn't me; I'm better than this." Then go harder for thirty to forty seconds. Very often you'll surprise yourself with what you've got left in the tank.

Be aware of what your thoughts were just before you started losing it. So often those thoughts are about other's performances. Often thoughts of race outcomes will bring on a losing-it episode. Try the thirty- to forty-second test, and then bring your thoughts back to the process, the job at hand. All of a sudden, you're back in the race.

Smart people start their diet at the supermarket. You can't eat what you don't buy.

Becoming a Winner

These are short stories about winners I've known. They're not all triathletes, but they're all people who have motivated me along the way.

Peggy

Peggy was a nickname given to her by her twin sister many years ago. Peggy and her sister were orphans. She told the story of begging others in the orphanage for the skin off their apples. Some of the other kids were sent fruit by relatives, but Peggy and her sister missed out on this privilege.

When they reached fourteen, the girls were sent to neighbouring cattle properties to work as nanny/ housemaids. They worked in the country until they were eighteen, when they were released and allowed to return to their home town to live with their dad.

Peggy worked as a waitress in the local pub, and her sister took up nursing. Both met men and were married at around twenty-one. Peggy moved to Brisbane with her new husband, and her sister lived out her life in the country town.

Peggy and her husband worked hard raising a family. Her husband worked as a truck driver, and when the kids were old enough, Peggy worked as a waitress. They built the family home themselves and, as the years went by, invested in another house and then another. Lots of hard work, long hours, and thrifty living paid off.

Peggy's husband died when she was in her late fifties. He was older than she was. It was hard, but she had to move on—more hard work and thrifty living.

Peggy is approaching ninety years. She's my mother. She's the most active eighty-plus -year-old you'll ever meet. She walks for miles and dances several days a week.

She's recently sold a couple of properties, and as her eldest son, I have sat in on her consultations with a financial adviser. Just to convert his financial-adviser's talk into plain English: it's time for her to let her money work for her, rather than her working for it. I'm so happy for her to be able to live without relying on government handouts and to be able to enjoy her retirement in comfort, all because of her own hard work.

When I was young, my vision of a millionaire was sports cars, speed boats, and beautiful women. I had no idea it was very likely to be a little old lady in a Corolla, who shops for every bargain available.

In my eyes, she's a winner—her resilience, her confidence, her long-term view, and the inspiration she's been to so many of us. You don't have to be an athlete to be a winner. Having a vision and pursuing it relentlessly while living a full life that inspires others along the way, in my eyes, makes you a winner.

She'll never lose her thrifty ways. When you've been hungry, you learn not to waste.

Man was not meant to be at rest. If fitness goes, the mind is not far behind.

Kieren

For ten years I had a small bike shop in Brisbane. It was a little "hole in the wall" type of shop where I went to recover from my training. When I started the shop, I had no competition in a five-kilometre radius. Over the years, four other shops moved in on my territory. I was faced with the option of spending lots of money, moving into bigger premises, or getting out and doing something else.

When I started the shop, I was a bike-shop owner, who did a bit of coaching on the side. And ten years later, I was a triathlon coach who ran a bike shop on the side.

My shop was five hundred metres up the road from the pool where the great Kieren Perkins trained. As part of his training, Kieren did some cycling. I supplied him with a custom-made racing bike.

Shortly before the Atlanta Olympics, the pool was burgled, and Kieren's bike was stolen. Maybe Kieren went to Atlanta angry.

About four weeks after Kieren had won his second gold medal in the fifteen hundred-metre event, he came into the shop to be measured up for his replacement bike.

We had one of the most inspirational conversations I have ever had with an athlete.

I am always interested in what athletes think. As I've touched on earlier, I believe once you're fit, 70 per cent of performance comes from the mind.

Kieran told me of his long term goal. A goal he'd had for more than ten years. He approached his training, his life, with a purpose driven by a vision which he could turn on whenever he needed a reason to do the right thing.

He owned his goal, he could sight that goal anytime he needed to be strong, be committed.

When he said that, I got goose pimples. When would he have made that goal—when he was thirteen, fifteen? That's a long-term view. What would we all achieve if we set goals and held onto them for ten or twelve years?

Kieren came so close to achieving his goal of three gold medals. He retired from swimming with two gold and one silver medal in the Olympic fifteen hundred-metre swim.

With the ability to hold a goal for that long and to pursue it with dedication like he has, he'll be successful in whatever field he enters. Nothing can stand in the way of that sort of energy.

If you keep believing what you've been believing, you'll keep achieving what you've been achieving.

Mark

When I did my first Ironman, I did 13.50. I wasn't happy. I didn't feel like a winner at all. When Mark did his first Ironman in Taupo 2005, he did 13.50, and he was a winner.

See, in November 2003, Mark was out having a run one afternoon, training for the Coomera Half Ironman. An idiot driving too fast around a corner lost control of his car in the gravel and mounted the footpath, driving Mark through a picket fence and running over him.

Mark was rushed to hospital having lost so much blood that doctors patched him up but would not operate on him until he was strong enough to handle it. They thought he wouldn't make it to the operation.

He gained some strength and looked like he might be worth the gamble. He had three broken ribs, a punctured lung, and he lost half his liver and a kidney. They managed to fit eighteen units of blood into him and around one hundred stitches.

It takes more than that to kill a Cyco. His wife tried to make a claim on his personal accident/trauma policy and was told this didn't fit their criteria of trauma! When Mark was able, he was wheeled into the Suncorp Insurance office, where he lifted his shirt and showed them his stitched up stomach, crisscrossed with scars. He asked them, "Does this look like trauma?" They paid.

Doctors told Mark he would never be the same and to expect a three-year recovery. By September 2004 he felt he was ready to try himself in a Half Ironman at Yeppoon. He did that okay and then set his sights on the Taupo New Zealand Ironman 2005.

He raced his first Ironman in Taupo, finishing in thirteen hours and fifty minutes. He was a Winner. Mark has a busy life and travels a lot with work. He doesn't have time to train for triathlon but cycles lots and has just returned from a five-day bike tour of the Rockies, cycling up to 12,000 feet.

Winning has more to do with getting up when you've been knocked down than fast times.

Your belief determines your action, and your action determines your results. Better feedback from your results generally improves your attitude and future new results. But first you have to believe.

Sherilee

Many of the athletes who come through my door have not had a lot of background in any one sport. Sometimes they have no experience at the sports involved, but they have this burning desire to test themselves.

Sherilee had completed another triathlon squad's beginner course. She had done all she was going to do with the other group when she came along to one of my sessions. She was shy and overweight.

She was tall, around 178 to 180 centimetres and over one hundred kilograms. She was unfit and tried to avoid attention.

One thing that became apparent early in her training was her ability to focus on a task and her willingness to give things her best shot. As part of her training, I helped her outline a diet plan and asked how things were going often enough for her to feel I was watching and encouraging.

She asked if I'd train her for the Gold Coast Half Ironman. We had a large group training for it and had enough of a range of abilities to divide the group into two levels. The lesser-developed group was mainly girls with a couple of guys. That group bonded so well they would socialise together, train together, and look out for each other.

They argued, they celebrated victories, and they laughed a lot. They all raced the Half Ironman. It was an extreme day, hot and 36 degrees Celsius; windy on the bike; and steamy hot on the run. The spirit in that group was so strong that every one waited at the finish line for each other to cross.

Finishing that event in the toughest of conditions, with a 100 per cent finish rate and a 95 per cent qualification rate for the full Ironman, defined the "new guys" as full "Cycos." It wasn't a qualification enforced by anyone else but themselves. They felt they had made it.

Sherilee trained as hard as our best athletes. In fact, I'm sure her attendance rate at training sessions was 100 per cent. In her whole life, I'm sure she hadn't been as focused on any one thing as much as this.

The kilos seemed to drop off her tall frame. No one was more disciplined.

When she stood at the start line at Forster, I felt very proud for her. Here she was, not a natural athlete by any stretch of the imagination but ready to put her heart and soul on the line.

She swam the time I was expecting, had a quick transition, and got into the bike. She gained places all through the second half of the bike, the stage where the mind has to overrule the legs.

It was the run where she stamped her authority on the race. When she started the race, she weighed ninety-two kilograms. She ran down fourteen men in the same age group as her—thirty-five to thirty-nine. And later, when we looked up the results, she had run down fourteen men in the forty to forty-four age group.

I'd say the guys who were run down by Sherilee didn't exactly feel like winners. But in my book, Sherilee was definitely a winner.

Great thinking attracts great results; mediocre thinking attracts mediocre results.

Alex

My wife used to think I was wasting time posting on Transitions (a triathlon forum). In fact, she thinks I'm wasting time any time I'm not out there sweating in the hot Queensland sun. I think I've spoiled her. My average day starts at 4:30 a.m. I'm either out training at 5:00 a.m. or at the pool coaching at 5:30 a.m. After I have coached the squad, I train myself, usually swim or sometimes swim, and then do intervals on the wind trainer.

After that, I either write training programs or articles, on an easy day, or work at landscaping projects. In the evening, I answer all of my e-mails and catch up with my office work, knocking off at about 7:00 p.m. Anything less, and she thinks I'm getting soft.

If I hadn't wasted my time on Transitions, I would not have met Alex. The amazing thing is that he almost bought a block of land just down the road from me a year earlier, and we could have been neighbours.

Alex contacted me after reading some of my posts and some of the critical comments I attracted on Trannies. It seemed that some of the Trannies folk disagreed with whatever I said without evaluating the content.

Anyway, it was a good day for both of us. They say good horses make good trainers; the same goes for coaches.

Who would have ever heard of John Carew, if Kieren Perkins had not walked into his swim school?

From the first contact I had with Alex, I read, "honesty, intelligence, cool head, responsible, committed." They say you only get one chance to make a first impression. I am usually guided by gut instinct.

Alex had trained with me for twelve months, in that time he dropped over twenty kilogram. (I'm not a details person. He'll probably tell you it's 23.62 kilograms.) He's like that; he likes details. Me, I like the big picture and the feel of things.

Apart from his dramatic weight loss, his athleticism and personality have changed. He's gone from being a lone trainer searching the Internet for new training ideas and the latest equipment to a Cyco, a valued teammate who can be relied on for his dedication and courage.

After the first year of training, Alex reduced his Half Ironman time by one hour and fourteen minutes. We both looked forward to his next Ironman event, Busselton, in December '07. The previous year it was his first Ironman in a time of 13.50. I wasn't going to be surprised if he were to take four hours off that

After Alex raced the Western Australian Ironman at Busselton, one year after his first Ironman, his finish time was nine hours and fifty-one minutes. I think this is an international record for the greatest improvement in one year.

In Ironman triathlon, attitude is everything.

Alex is already a winner, and he has lots more to achieve.

Life is a grindstone, and whether it grinds you down or polishes you up is for you alone to decide.

Minnie

A lot of our current squad members know Minnie as a cheeky, funny girl who loves her training and always has a joke to share. Most don't know Minnie's story.

When she was a little girl, she walked in callipers until she was five years old to straighten her legs (like Forrest Gump).

I met her when I started coaching her boyfriend. He asked me to write her a program. I hesitated at the time. They had moved up from Sydney, and the group Minnie had done some running with had her injured often. To be honest, I thought she wouldn't handle the training. She looked too frail.

He persisted, so eventually I wrote her one, concentrating on her swimming and cycling with just enough running to hold some sort of run technique.

She was an enthusiastic trainer, always there and keen to do whatever she had to do. Over a couple of months, she proved to be tougher than her boyfriend. He was a bit of a skirt when things were tough. She had the sort of attitude where nothing would stop her. The harder the workout and the tougher the conditions, the harder she became.

The squad was training for the Australian Ironman in Forster 96. Minnie asked if I thought she could do it. I really didn't want to injure her. I agreed to train her for it but told her we would be aiming at building most of her fitness in the swim and bike, while using just enough running to get by.

Race day arrived, and the squad did well. It seemed that the farther Minnie went, the stronger she became mentally. The squad had the fastest bike in five categories and second fastest in four others. We had eleven Hawaii qualifiers.

Minnie won the eighteen to twenty-four category by fifty-five minutes.

She qualified for Hawaii 96. While we trained running on forest trails, she had an accident. She twisted her ankle and broke it, twelve weeks out from Hawaii. We had to carry her out of the forest.

She was devastated; her dream shattered.

She had one week off training. When the swelling went down, the doctors fitted a fibreglass cast to her leg so she could still swim and water run.

When the squad trained long on Sundays, I would prepare a script for Minnie, setting out length of climbs, heart rates, frequency of climbs, and so on. She rode with a Velcro strap holding her cast to her cycle shoe. She did up to six-hour sessions on the trainer and up to two-hour, water-run sessions.

Five weeks out from Hawaii, the doctors removed her cast. She had to learn to walk, jog, and then run on it. We kept her to the grass and kept up the water running. Before leaving for Hawaii, I had her run a one-hour road run, the following week a ninety-minute run, a then a two-hour run on the road. That was three runs in the twelve-week lead up to the Hawaii Ironman.

She raced Hawaii 96. We had a mental preparation strategy worked out. She would reward herself for everyone she passed in the run. It was always going to be a run. We had visualised the whole thing unfolding over and over. Always running and continually passing people. Passing one at a time was good. But when she passed two walking together, she gave herself a little reward affirmation.

Minnie finished in the top five in her category (in Hawaii they recognise top five in every category). She had the second fastest run in her category, with three runs on the road in the previous twelve weeks.

The following year she raced Forster 97 in the next category: twenty-five to twenty-nine. She won that as well and raced Hawaii again in '97.

Minnie had achieved much more than she ever had imagined possible. She had split from the boyfriend (who, although big and strong, was as soft as butter). She moved back to Sydney and, after some time away from sport, took up running again.

Quite a few marathons later, she found herself drawn back to Queensland, where she entered a one hundred-kilometre running race. It was the Australian 100-kilometre championship. She won by hours. She raced the Australian one hundred-kilometre champs in 2003, 2004, and 2005. She was unbeaten for three years and set a fastest time of ten hours and sixteen seconds.

Her body was not really designed for ultra running. Personally I don't think any bodies are. After a few lengthy injuries, Minnie decided to get back into a sport that balances the load over the whole body, so she came back to the Cycos.

Welcome back, Minnie. I'm proud to have one of the toughest people I have ever met back in the squad.

Everyone has fear in them; it all depends on what you do with that fear that makes you a hero or a coward.

Body Maintenance Versus Body Repairs

During an interview, one of Australia's best known pro-triathletes stated he spent as much time on body maintenance, massage, stretching, and so on as he spent training.

I've always advocated preventative maintenance rather than repairs. I guess that attitude comes from having owned earthmoving equipment and trucks in a past life. With expensive equipment, maintenance is almost a religion.

Some of my athletes have assumed I am anti-physiotherapy. The truth is I am very pro-physiotherapists. But I don't recommend using them the way many athletes do—waiting until something goes wrong, such as an injury.

I suggest using a physio to check you out before you're injured. Get the physio to check your core strength and give you the exercises to correct weaknesses. Have him or her check your flexibility, and then get the best advice on which stretches you need to do to correct your inflexibility.

Lots of athletes training for an ironman position all of their massages into the last six to eight weeks, trying to undo all of the muscular tension they've built up over the previous six months.

I have always suggested athletes either pay to have a massage or full-body acupuncture once every two weeks. If money is short, and it often is after buying all the triathlon toys, athletes should learn self-massage or team up with a friend and massage each other. It's not really that hard. The receiver can guide the one giving the massage as to how hard, a little higher/lower, and so on.

I've gone for periods as long as three years without a massage. During that time, I've had acupuncture once per week. It doesn't hurt as much as a massage, and it releases the tension from any sore muscles. My Chinese herbalist/acupuncturist balances any of my systems that may be slightly less than 100 per cent with acupuncture or herbal preparations. They may taste awful, but I rarely get sick or injured.

Yoga is a nice way to maintain flexibility and put a little balance back into your busy life. Both acupuncture and yoga aim to balance the flow of chi (energy—life force). Rather than spend extra hours cycling or running, include an hour of yoga in your program to help keep your life balanced and very likely prevent an injury later in the season. Another benefit is it's possible to have a wife or partner join you at a yoga class and help to balance the training and relationship.

All of the muscles you're going to use in your next race are told what to do by a nervous system that connects to your spine. The stresses absorbed by your spine during a two-hour running session are greater than the average non-athlete would experience in a month. It's very important to use the services of a good chiropractic doctor as often as the budget will allow. Spinal alignment is critical to good performance. You may get away without attention in this area when you're in your twenties, but as you get older, you'll really feel the difference. When selecting a chiro, seek out one who practices applied kinesiology to help correct a lot more imbalances like dietary, emotional, and subconscious belief systems. It is no coincidence that Mark Allen, six-time winner of the Hawaii Ironman had his kinesiologist travel with him to Hawaii each year.

Become good at balancing the work-rest ratio. The stress-healing ratio is definitely the secret to longevity in this sport. After all, most of us are not in this sport for the prize money. We're in it for the fun, health benefits, friendships, and personal development brought on by preparing ourselves and testing ourselves.

Don't underestimate the value of body maintenance and balance.

You wouldn't be human if you didn't feel nervous before a competition.

How Would You Live If You Only Had Five Months Left?

A man who had a recent heart transplant said that every minute of every day, he enjoys what he has, and he lives in total appreciation of what he has.

Why didn't he live like that before?

Every day that we wake up, we have so much. If it's fine, we can enjoy the sunshine. If it's rainy, we can enjoy the rain. The journey to work can be enjoyable. Look at the faces of all the people you see along the way. Every face tells a story. Let your imagination unravel that story. Listen to the sounds. Some of the simplest things can be the most beautiful sounds—birds singing, kids playing, or rain on the roof.

When we trained in the Lake at the Gold Coast, the water was clean, the temperature was mild, and the morning was beautiful. What a great place to train.

Then when we cycled over to the hinterland mountains for a climbing workout—three or four climbs up Springbrook mountain and through the rainforest, with waterfalls running down through the forest and under the road. What a fantastic place to cycle.

Halfway up one of the climb efforts, four red Ferraris drove past. What a sound. There is something pure and original with the sound of a Ferrari, an MGB, a Ducati, or a Harley. After the fastest guys had done their four climbs, we all regrouped and rode back to Robina. We had a roaring headwind. But it was still fantastic, our tired legs pushing into a thirty kilometres-per-hour wind. It wasn't far. It was just like riding into Hawi on the Big Island.

Far too often, people miss some of the best experiences because they don't live in the moment. They think of what could go wrong, what someone else thinks, and what someone else is doing at the time.

If you were told that you have five months to live, would you live differently? In most cases the answer is yes. Why is that so?

If you'd live differently if you only had five months to go, why don't you live like that now? Do you fear running out of money? Do you fear looking like a fool?

If you're not living your life to the fullest, right now, you do look like a fool. You're not going to get another chance. You have to take every opportunity to enjoy what you have right now.

If it's a fear of running out of money, you have nothing to worry about. Living in the moment doesn't cost any more than living in fear. Just learn to enjoy everything that fills your life. Like the heart-transplant man said, every minute of every day.

When you race in the swim, just swim—no other thoughts. On the bike, just ride it hard, and smile as though you're enjoying it. We do this sport because we love it. It's supposed to be fun. It is possible to enjoy cycling into a headwind and riding in the rain or the searing heat.

How often do we see people running who look like they've lost a million bucks? If you've done the training, and if you're focusing on running the four hundred metre in front of you, no matter how tired you are, it can be fun. I don't mean fun like blowing out the candles on your birthday cake. I mean satisfying-type fun like when you've predicted something that has actually happened.

That's how it can be on race day. You can predict how it's going to be—fast, strong, and focused on the moment. That's how it'll be, and then it'll be fun.

Dedication ultimately proves to be better than ability.

It's Good to Be a Triathlete

Every week when I read the weekly reports from the athletes on my training programs, I want the details of performance, health, feelings, and so on. The news is not always good. Every workout or every big weekend of training is not going to produce PBs or even good experiences. The road to the top is not a straight line. There are a few dips along the way, but the general trend is upward.

It's good to be triathletes and not wild-west gunfighters. The gunfighter who has a bad day doesn't get to analyse his performance and tell someone about it. The Samurai swordsman who lives into his forties has had an incredible run of good days.

Let's face it, good days come from preparing well, from learning from the bad days, and from being better prepared next time. Put behind you the analysis that follows a bad race or disappointing training day. It is only one day in a fantastic life.

We are privileged to live a life of beautiful sunrises, shared with a great bunch of people who'll help you out if you need it and shoot you down if you become too self-centred. If you have had a bad race or a couple of poor training sessions, do a bit of self-analysis. Ask advice from a more experienced athlete or your coach. Then put it behind you, and look forward to the great days this life produces.

Have you ever noticed how triathletes like to talk about themselves? We all do it. You'll become a lot more interesting to listen to if the only thing you do say about yourself is the answers to questions. Keep them short and to the point. Your friends and family really don't want a detailed analysis of your bad race or less than satisfying training day.

Friends and family will be far more interested in your goals and plans for the future than what went wrong over the weekend. Enjoy your PBs, and record them in your diary. Always record what went right, learn from what went wrong, and to move on.

Every sunrise is the promise of another great day; leave the past in the shadows of yesterday.

**If you have a strong enough reason,
you can do anything.**

All People Have a Ten-Hour Ironman in Them

A ten-hour Ironman is made up of six hundred efficient minutes. Any time you spend being inefficient simple adds to your total. Whether you end up with six hundred minutes or seven hundred minutes or even eight hundred and forty minutes can and will be determined by how efficient you become in your preparation.

So all training, whether it's off-season maintenance training or the sharpening up just before your next major race needs to be directed at developing maximum efficiency.

Swimming is the classic example of how efficiency can help you improve. Lowering your number of strokes to complete a length of your training pool is the first step. Your swim coach can offer suggestions on how to improve this and give you feedback on what's not working for you. Head position— relax your neck and lower your head, and instantly your body lays on top of the water instead of dragging through it. Learn to "feel the water." The fastest swimmers feel the water and hold onto it as they swim by. Develop several "gears" in your swimming. Many poor swimmers have only one speed in arm turnover rate. To react to varying conditions in the swim, you need several different speeds.

Always be practicing when in the pool rather than training. Golfers and tennis players always practice. Our game is as heavily dependent on technique as theirs is.

Great cyclists have done thousands of hours in the saddle. Most of that time was spent learning to roll the gears with light pedal pressure. They have to do some hard pushing, but the bulk of their hours are spent building pedalling efficiency and conditioning the muscles to build endurance into them. Endurance at a muscular level is not something that can be rushed. It can only be built a little at a time, a bit like building a huge cathedral out of hand-sized bricks.

Some of the fastest female Ironman cyclists are small women. Often they weigh around fifty-two to fifty-four kilograms, yet they have often ridden under five hours for the Ironman bike. They all have one thing in common; they spin along at higher than ninety reps per minute. They don't have the strength of the bigger, stronger guys, but they get there with pedalling efficiency. Yet with this result so easily seen, we see big, strong male athletes grinding along at eighty to eighty-five reps per minute and not riding anywhere near as fast.

Every time you take your bike out, do it for a purpose. Learn to pedal smoothly and with light pedal pressure. Every cyclist I have passed in the final forty kilometres of the Hawaii Ironman bike course has been pedalling inefficiently.

I have heard experts say you shouldn't change a runner's technique; they'll become injured. This is bullshit. Running technique is as important as swimming technique in determining final times. Simple changes imprinted into the mind with run drills can drastically change the outcome in a long race. But be careful; you have to allow the new technique to become a habit. Any time the old style is practiced, it keeps the old way alive. When you learn something new, you cannot ever allow yourself to go back to doing it the old way.

Most poor runners don't have good posture. Good core strength is the foundation for good posture. Look at the posture of dancers and gymnasts. Little kids learn to stand correctly and run correctly; their parents have unlearned this simple skill. Adults very often need to relearn how to stand and walk efficiently. I can sit in a cafe and watch the people walk by and pick the poor bastards who would be lousy runners, simply by the way they walk.

A good coach can simply give you different thoughts to hold, which will change the way you run.

Every run is a practice session in efficiency, especially when you run tired. Holding it together when you're exhausted is often the key to that great time you're aiming at.

If every minute spent training is a minute spent on improving your efficiency, when you next step up to a start line, you'll need fewer minutes to get to the finish line.

You can have anyone, no matter how famous, tell you that you can do something. But if you don't believe in yourself, then that is a real battle.

Playing with the Cards You've Been Dealt

When I walk into the pool on a Monday night to coach the swim session, the first thing I do is read the faces. I look for the "look" that indicates "ready to go" or "beam me up, Scotty."

I'll have a session written, ready to go. But if the faces are saying, "I really wish I was home watching the channel seven news," I go to plan B. Plan B is a lighter session with more emphasis on technique and drill work rather than trying to wring the last drop of energy out of my players.

There'll be some who are ready to fire up and some who are struggling. We're all individuals. Some of the squad members were still struggling after a WA IM one early December. Those athletes dug to the bottom of the barrel. It takes a long time to put back the emotional energy, or chi, that is used in a really courageous performance. That's why top marathoners have only got two good races in them each year.

For my online athletes, this decision is up to you. The squad athletes can't hide what their bodies are telling me. But if you live in another city, look in the mirror. Your face will tell you if you should push yourself or back off and substitute a session with one of the easier sessions.

I've found there are times in the moon's cycle when athletes bounce back quicker from a heavy Sunday session. Keep track in your diary of how you bounce back. A pattern starts to emerge.

Often only swimming one thousand metres is going to be more beneficial than grinding out a three thousand-metre session. You may just be wasting some of your chi to drive yourself through the bigger session.

When I write the programs, I write them to suit a perfect world where athletes get eight hours sleep each night and have a good balanced diet. These athletes take their supplements, don't drink excessively, and have harmonious relationships.

Do you know anyone like this? The goal is to get as close to this as possible, but it's hard at times. You may have to adjust your training a little to fit into your life.

If you train in my Brisbane squad, I'll adjust the work according to your body language or your feedback.

It's important to remember that it's not soft to adjust a training plan to suit your energy levels; it's smart.

If there weren't nerves from the pressure, atmosphere, and build-up to the race, it would be pretty dull.

Swim Faster By Swimming on Top of the Water

Free advice is one of the most plentiful commodities in triathlon. The supply is even bigger in Ironman training groups. I love reading the posts on some forums, where anonymous people hand out all sorts of advice. Often based on what they've read somewhere or heard somewhere.

One of the best ones I've heard is that triathletes don't ever need to kick.

People who swim well, swim often. The top swimmers use part of every swim session to work on each part of their stroke. Sadly for some this means including some kicking drills in each session. Many don't like it. Very often the things you don't like doing are the very things that you should be doing more of.

The argument I've heard is that most of your propulsion in a long-distance swim comes from the upper body. I don't dispute that for a minute. Triathletes need to be able to kick effectively for streamlining. An effective kick will put the swimmer into a better position to reduce drag. Seventy per cent of the athlete's power goes into overcoming drag. Only 30 per cent of the triathlete's power is going into producing forward movement. It just makes good sense to reduce drag first.

Most of the swimmers I've worked with have not had a swimming background. Many did not start swim training until they were in their mid-thirties. I personally didn't do any swim training until I was thirty-six. In my first race, I only beat three people out of the water over five hundred metres.

I encourage every triathlete who is not happy with his or her swim time to incorporate some kicking drills in every workout. You will get results. Kicking up and down a pool for hundreds of metres will break your heart. I suggest that three hundred metres of every session be done as twelve metres of kicking and then twelve metres of freestyle, repeated over and over.

The idea here is to do enough kicking to use the kicking muscles effectively. This is done with the arms extended out the front, relaxed and straight, balancing the swimmer in the water. At the end of each twelve-metre kick, with the arms out front and the feet applying downward pressure on the water, the swimmer is lying on top of the water. He or she then swims twelve metres starting in the correct body position. Swimming feels easy (less drag).

What makes this kick drill more effective is the arms are out front balancing the body—the neck is relaxed, and the eyes look straight down. The kick is a relaxed flutter, with the legs close together (this is not done with much force). The feet are loose, and the legs are unlocked at the knees and ankles. The feet don't extend up out of the water, and they don't extend down deeper into the water than the swimmer's chest does. (The feet cannot be seen from a front-on position. They don't extend outside of the circle that the chest and shoulders pass through the water)

When the kicker needs a breath, a single arm stroke can be taken. (If the swimmer keeps one eye in the water, the head is not lifted out of position.) The head must remain in line with the centre line of the body, neck relaxed.

To get started on becoming balanced in the water, practice a simple drill. Push off from the wall of the pool with arms out straight (keep them relaxed) and head between the upper arms looking straight down. Now kick with the loosest legs and softest feet. Just go as far as you can, slowly releasing your breath until it's all gone. Swim back to the wall, and repeat this drill, trying to go further each time. You'll get used to how good swimmers feel in the water—lying on top of it. (The arms must stay out in front to balance the body.)

The next step is to kick off almost as far as you can, and then add two freestyle strokes, without lifting your head.

The time spent learning to swim on top of the water will be more effective than ploughing up and down with a pull buoy between your legs. This is not strenuous work and can be fitted in after other workouts when you're tired. It's more of a mental exercise than a physical one. It's about "feel for the water." It's about swimming with the water instead of against it.

There has to be a reason why skinny eleven-year-old girls can outswim lots of mature-aged triathletes with three times the strength. The reason is position and balance in the water. Some of the forum posters will never get it.

The best way to predict the future is to create it.

Don't Overthink the Swim

Analysis paralysis is an epidemic in triathlon. We read the planned strategies posted by guys on triathlon forums. The advice offered by anonymous experts on the same forums. They go to so much detail—so many grams of this, so many litres per hour, or the precise number of gels for the bike. It all reads like the secret to success. Unfortunately, after the race is run and the dust has settled, those detailed plans often didn't work out as planned.

Most of the athletes I meet have taken up swimming as adults. They've missed the technique-building period before the age of fifteen, which is believed to be the best time to lay the foundations for elite swimming.

Our adult starters are so keen to get it right, they'll do anything or buy anything that can help them become competitive swimmers. I've found communication to be the secret to getting adult swimmers to loosen up and develop their strokes. The main obstacle is too much information is available. The athlete becomes confused. Some of the heavily marketed swim-technique programs often confuse athletes by getting them to try to be too technical. Most adult swimmers don't have the flexibility to body roll as an elite swimmer does.

One of the simplest ways to get faster is to work on the part of the swim stroke that is going to give the most forward propulsion. The part I refer to is the portion of the stroke after the catch has been executed and the fingers point to the bottom of the pool. From here the large muscles in the back take over, and the force is applied with the portion of the arm from the elbow down to the fingertips.

This is exactly the part of the arm that pushes you ahead as you paddle a surfboard. Did you ever notice that when you paddle a surfboard, you don't analyse your stroke? You just grab hold of the water and push against it. You have a fast arm turnover because you want to get out there before the next wave pushes you back. Another thing you'll notice is that you're having fun. It's easy.

Now, if we could just carry the mental states we have on our surfboards into the pool. Bring the simplicity of the movement and the fun aspect of surfboard paddling into the pool—no analysis, just doing. When you're having fun, there's no muscular tension; your arms and hands are loose. When you're focusing on every detail of Michael Phelps's swim stroke and trying to emulate it, you create muscular tension.

Now look at the kids in the swim squad at the local pool. They're cruising up and down the pool with ease, no tension. Almost no thoughts going on in their minds. They're training hard and having fun. And they're going faster than most adult swimmers go.

If we can learn to have fun while we train, our times are going to come down. The same thing when we race. The simplest thoughts are most productive. By the time we get to race day, we should have practiced technique so much that we no longer have to think about it. Visualise a surfboard between your hands when they enter the water. This ensures they enter in the right place. Then just grab the water and push.

Bumblebees and Racehorses

A few years ago a group of scientists developed an interest in bumblebees. The scientists reckoned that these little insects held some secrets of flight that might provide some answers to questions about operating in space. After all, they asked, how could such small wings produce efficient lift for a relatively large and hairy torso? And how could a round body and flight position that violated many principles of aerodynamics move so efficiently through the air?

After weeks of study, hypothesizing, scrutinizing, and examining, the scientists came to one conclusion: Bumblebees are not capable of flight. Fortunately, no one told the bumblebees. The silly insects go right on believing that flight is normal for them despite what the best minds in the scientific world know as fact. We can learn a lot from the bumblebee. The single most critical piece of this sporting puzzle is believing in yourself and your capacity to succeed. "If you think you can or you think you can't," automobile manufacturer Henry Ford said, "you're probably right." The bumblebee thinks it can fly. Actually, the thought of anything else never even crosses its tiny mind. It just keeps flying.

Then there's the racehorse. The physiology of equine athletes is similar to that of human athletes, and they are trained in much the same manner as a runner. They use heart-rate monitors, train with intervals and endurance, follow a periodization plan, and eat a diet designed to enhance performance. Psychologically, racehorses differ a great deal from the human athlete. They never question their training preparations. When it comes time for a workout designed by their trainers, they do it without wondering if it's enough. They don't go out in the morning and put in a few extra junk miles for "insurance." They don't worry and fret after a poor performance. Stable life goes on as usual. On race day, racehorses are nervous, just as human athletes are. They know what is about to happen, but they don't magnify the tension by comparing themselves with the other horses ("look at the legs on that stud!"). Instead, they are very purposeful in their approach to training and racing. There is but one reason for everyday existence—to get faster. If the horse is physically strong and the trainer is smart, this happens.

If you are to succeed in the sport you have chosen, the first thing you must do is believe in yourself just as the bumblebee does. Without this, all of the science in the world won't do any good. You must also have a purposeful, racehorse trust in your training. Continuously second guessing and changing training direction after every race are sure ways to fail. Think like a bumblebee; train like a horse.

**If you really want what you want,
there's always a way to create it.**

If You Want to Swim Faster, Get the Feeling

Most of us were introduced to this sport as adults, many of us coming from non sporty backgrounds. Most of us are keen to learn as much as we can. Too many of us simply try too hard and over intellectualise the simple tasks of swimming, cycling and

I've seen many research every aspect of each of these sports. Then analyse what they do and end up with analysis paralysis. The more we analyse our moves, the more we control our moves, and the more muscular tension we build up. This inhibits natural, free movement.

One of the hardest jobs for a coach of mature-aged athletes is communicating the message in a way that is so simple that it cannot be analysed. In the swim, if we become aware of our bodies from our fingertips to our toes (not tight or under any amount of tension but simply aware of the length from an extended arm down to a relaxed, pointed set of toes—the greatest length possible) then it's possible to push off the wall in this lengthened, relaxed state and float for five to eight metres without any other propulsion than the push.

That's the first step in getting "the feeling." When you glide along in the water in a balanced position with an arm out front, the next step is to swim with soft hands. Apply the same amount of pressure on the water that you would apply to a dog when you pat his head or stroke his back. No harder. Swimming with soft hands allows you to feel the water. It also gets rid of the muscular tension that slows down your recovery and makes you look "mechanical" in the water.

So, we have one hand out front; we're aware right down to our soft, relaxed toes; and we have soft hands. Next part is to recover after pushing through, with your fingers hanging like you're letting the water drip off them. Lead the recovery with your wrist (as though there is no hand attached). The recovery portion of the stroke is a "one" in muscular tension, on a scale from one to ten.

So, now we're floating along, aware of our full length, with soft hands, and we're recovering as though we have no hands attached to our wrists. Now we need to propel ourselves along. If we take on the belief that we're pushing ourselves along instead of pulling ourselves along, we'll be applying the pressure to the water in the right part of the stroke. Imagine there's a wall right under our body, running down the middle. Don't let your hands cross under you. Keep the fingers pointing to the bottom, and don't let your thumbs touch that imaginary wall.

So far I have not mentioned keeping up with the faster swimmers in your lane. I have not mentioned beating the guy in the next lane. I have not mentioned time bases or records. An adult swimmer must learn to swim loose before he or she learns to go faster. Remember that if it were golf or tennis, you would not be training, you'd be practicing. To make real progress, an adult swimmer needs to practice often, as often as possible. Six sessions a week is not too much. The sessions do not need to be long; one thousand metres is enough to reinforce the feeling we're cultivating.

When I get new athletes in the squad, I have them do as many sessions as we can manage, aiming at achieving this feeling in the water. I would rather they swim in a lane slower than they feel they're capable of holding on in. Your progress will be limited if you spend all your time in the pool holding on. You need to swim slow enough to be able to breathe both sides. And when you do breathe, you need to keep one eye in the water. If this is difficult at first, stick at it, because it will feel easy and natural within six to eight sessions. Use fins when you swim, if necessary, to master this skill. To swim a straight line in open water, you must be capable of breathing bilaterally.

If you get into the water, feeling anxious about how you're going to keep up, you're already on the wrong foot. The self-talk you use is so important in setting you up for a good day. Try "let it be easy," "I'm here to practice perfect technique," "I'm here to feel the water support me," "push myself forward," and "soft hands, loose toes."

Every emotion you experience is a direct response to a thought, not to the world around you.

You Only Swim in the Top Three Feet

Often young athletes are discouraged by the few Hawaii qualifying spots available to each category. It's got to be hard to get in; otherwise, people wouldn't value the chance to race there. Racing in Hawaii is a privilege and a hard-earned right. It's harder to get into an Australian swimming team for the World Champs.

One of the guys pointed out that at the Australian Ironman this year, in the thirty to thirty-four men's category, there were only seven Hawaii spots to cover 195 competitors. He was a bit discouraged.

It's my job to come up with the positive spin on any situation. In fact, I've been doing it so long that it's become a habit. I always see the best angle on any situation. It often annoys my wife when she's having a bit of a whinge.

If you take on the feeling that it's an almost impossible task to qualify when there are only seven spots for 195 athletes, you're pulling the rug from under your own feet. As soon as you doubt whether you can do it, you decrease the odds for the other guys. You're out of the race. "If you think you can, you can. If you think you can't, you're right again."

The "negative set" will now chime in with, "Be realistic." Being realistic is not a trademark of winners. Winners dream big. Winners make big plans and put them into action.

Some categories only have one qualifying spot. How many do you need?

When you swim in the ocean, you only swim in the top three feet. It doesn't matter how deep it is, you focus all of your energy on staying in the top three feet. You train yourself to be in the top three feet.

Taking on a top-three-feet mentality can affect everything in your life. Champions do not think like bottom feeders. They don't eat like bottom feeders; they don't approach their recovery like bottom feeders.

Swimming in the top three feet is a lifestyle. It won't necessarily change things overnight, but living this way will change your life. Racing with this attitude will maximise your chances of success. The world is full of people who aimed low, because they didn't feel worthy of aiming for the top.

As soon as the top-three-foot attitude is adopted, you'll start doing all the little things like a winner. An interesting phenomenon is winners don't become winners until they behave like winners. You don't just wake up one morning and find you've become a winner. As soon as you start living the life, you start the journey to becoming a winner.

**Your day doesn't create the mood;
your mood creates your day.**

Climb Like a Cyclist—Race Like a Triathlete

Let's face it; we're triathletes, not cyclists. Cyclists are completely different athletes with very different needs and talents. Some good cyclists have become good triathletes, but the transition is not an easy one.

Most of the athletes I deal with are interested in half and full Ironman events. In each case, the bike leg is a time trial. The physiological requirements for a triathlon time trial are very different from those of a cycling road race. In a road race, part of the game is to actually put yourself on the edge of blowing up, over and over in order to crack your competitors.

I know triathletes who train like this. Constantly smashing themselves to win a training session. They seldom take the same form into a race. Every surge and power spike they put in turns on their fast-twitch muscle fibres, which is exactly the opposite of what we want to happen if we're training for a time trial.

Great time trialists are very good at holding a high level of their maximum power output for an extended time. The best time trials usually have a steady power output spread over the whole distance. A time trial of one hour or less can be done at a higher percentage of their functional threshold power (FTP). The Ironman is usually raced at around 85 per cent of the athlete's FTP. The FTP is the average power the athlete can hold for twenty minutes.

To produce good Ironman bike times (and still be able to run off the bike), the athlete must become very good at extended efforts at or around 85 per cent of FTP. In layman's terms, that's around the level where you switch from being able to hold on to the point where you start to fade in an effort that is lasting for eight to ten minutes. It's important to hold this level on flat ground, but slight uphills can be used to great advantage. Long steady climbs of twenty to sixty minutes are ideal.

In working this important energy system, it's really important to pedal smoothly, rolling the gear along, rather than mashing a hard gear with excessive pedal pressure. Good cyclists can climb at a very fast rate and pedal smoothly. Staying in the optimum intensity range and still pedaling smoothly will not only help develop good time trialling technique but also save your knees. It's very possible to injure yourself on a bike without ever falling off.

Avoiding the trap of learning to pedal with really heavy pedal pressure is helpful when you want to run a marathon once you get off that bike.

A couple of years ago I watched the NZIM while my wife and several of my athletes raced. I stood on the hill where the athletes climb up from the lakeshore up and over the hill and out onto the open roads. Both Cameron

Brown and Jo Lawn stayed in their saddle, pedalling a high cadence. Lots of other athletes, with nowhere near the race results of Brown and Lawn, stood up and mashed a much bigger gear than the course champions did.

Every year I stand on the hill at Port Macquarie and watch athletes of all abilities climb it, three times in each direction. The fastest cyclists sit down and pedal a cadence of about seventy reps per minute; the battlers ride in or out of the saddle with anything from forty reps per minute to ninety reps per minute. A power meter can measure the pedal torque or pressure exerted on the pedals. I have turned athletes' performances around by having them become aware of their pedal pressure.

An example: Athlete A rode a very respectable bike time in IMNZ only to crash and burn spectacularly halfway through the run. Examining his recorded data revealed the secret. He had lots of spikes in his pedal pressure from an average of seven–nine up to nineteen–twenty (up to three times the pressure) with a heart rate change of only three to four beats. Racing by heart rate alone does not tell the whole story.

Once the athlete was made aware of these spikes in pedal pressure, he adjusted his cycling style and has made a huge leap forward in efficiency and, most importantly, his ability to run off the bike. The directions I gave him were to ride as if he had a block of wood under his accelerator pedal. When he came to a hill, his aim was to spin over the hill with little more effort than he would exert on the flat road. Then ride the downhill as hard as he could.

His average power steadily climbed with each one hundred-kilometre time trial he did, and his times dropped every time he tested himself.

Hope is the magic that energizes dreams and lets you live beyond historical thinking. There's never a good reason not to hope.

The Value of Time Trials in Ironman Training

About every month we do a one hundred-kilometre time trial. What I learn about the athlete is really important. But what the athlete learns is far more important. I've found the time trials to be one of the less popular workouts among some of the guys. Some love them; some find something else to do that day.

The solitude of the long time trial can really test the athlete's ability to stay focussed. This talent is of great importance in a longer race like the Ironman. The time trials are an important part of that physical preparation, conditioning the muscles to operate at a high level of intensity over a long time. This is so important for trouble-free running off the bike.

The other physical component often overlooked by athletes in their preparation is holding the aero position for hours at a time. It's just too easy to sit up in training and rest the neck and back. When your mates are going to look over your results, the desire to sit up and let a few seconds slip by is overruled by pride. We're not just conditioning legs here; its back, neck, and seat contact.

Controlling the ego is another important part of time trialling. It's just you against the clock. It's nice to be catching someone else, but learning to focus on putting power through those cranks is the key to faster times. You really can't evaluate your performance against anyone else. If someone who has been slower in the past comes past you, it doesn't mean you're not going well. They may be having a ripper performance.

I believe the greatest gains are mental. It gets lonely out there. It's going to be lonely on race day. The mental conditioning that comes from holding as high a power output as you can for three hours and more is money in the bank for race day.

Some people new to the sport are not sure how to handle the pain and discomfort involved in racing the clock for one hundred kilometres. Try looking forward to reaching the level where you can just tolerate it. Hold it there for as long as you can. There's a satisfaction to be gained by holding that level of discomfort. We're all competitive people, make this the competition: holding on longer than anyone else.

It's right at that edge where the winners operate. Regardless of how much background you have in the sport or how much talent you have, you'll become better at this by getting up to that edge and holding it longer than ever before. Some people fear that edge. They get close and then back off to just below. Or they think they're just below, but if they never go to the edge, they'll never know where it is.

Another talent that will come in handy on race day is to ride with an empty mind. No thoughts of how far to go. No thoughts of how far you've been. Just doing; just doing until it's done. A 9.30 Ironman is made up of 570 efficient minutes. The best time trials are as many efficient minutes as it takes you to get to the end. If you go into it with that mindset, simply produce enough efficient minutes to get to the end. Ride it one minute at a time.

This is the best mental training an Ironman athlete can do. Once this method of thinking is mastered, you start the bike, and before you know it, it's over. Then you have to turn on the mental strategy that you've practiced for the run.

Before every success is a dream, a goal, and a vision of the future.

Posture—Ever Give It a Thought?

Athletes training in my squad are exposed to a fair bit of core-strength work. When we do a two-week boot camp, we do a minimum of five hundred reps of core work every morning at 4:30 a.m. It's become a bit of a tradition. One of the exercises that challenges the new comers most is the scissors. Lie on your back, fold your arms, lift your shoulders and legs off the ground, and move the straight legs in a scissor-like fashion. Start at thirty seconds at a time and build. This is one of our most productive exercises, along with trunk twists and leg extensions.

We do the core work because most of my squad are training for either Ironman distance or Half Ironman. In both cases, the runner is hours into the race when the outcome is decided. If we look up the results of any Ironman race, in any category, the fastest runners take the prizes. The best runners always look pretty good, all the way through the run. They hold their posture.

Good runners have invested lots of hours into becoming good runners. Most of the best ones have done lots of track sessions involving drills and specific strength-building sessions. The ambitious ones who aspire to being great runners have also spent considerable time building strength specific to their needs as runners, not building beach muscles. Glute strength and the ability to hold the pelvis stable at any stage of the run require specific work.

If we stand and watch an Ironman race, that is, stand for ten to twelve hours watching the event unfold, we often suffer from lower back pain. This is simply standing around, not cycling for 180 kilometres and running a marathon ourselves. That lower back pain indicates poor posture in many cases; often poor posture as a result of poor core strength. Many of us simply do not have the strength or endurance to hold good posture for the length of time many will be racing. Many of those racing lack that strength and awareness of posture as well.

Apart from doing regular core-strength work as part of our training, becoming aware of good running posture actually is an important part of the road to racing at our potential. The Internet is full of video footage of very accomplished athletes running well. With the help of an experienced coach, it's possible to modify your run technique and improve your posture so that you're able to hold good posture, even when you're really tired.

If an athlete gives no thought to identifying what good posture actually feels like and then practices this feeling, under pressure, anything can happen. As soon as you lose control of your posture, you no longer apply pressure to the ground evenly and productively. Often stride length shortens, and leg turnover rate decreases. Both of these factors will mean your supporters will have to wait at the finish line longer than planned for you to turn up.

Every long run; every track session; and in fact, every time you run out the door, you have an opportunity to practice perfect running form. The old saying, "Practice makes perfect," is not actually correct; in fact, perfect practice makes perfect.

Champions are always prepared to do the hard yards, to live the lonely hours.

The Long Run

When training for an Ironman, the weekly long run is the most important workout of the week. In the actual race, your fortune is decided in the run. Mark Allen once said, "You swim and bike for show, and you run for the dough." If we look at the results of any category in an Ironman race, the fastest five runs are generally the fastest five overall places.

It's not uncommon for experienced Ironman competitors to run past other athletes who, over shorter distances, are better runners. One reason for this is a poorly executed nutrition plan. More Ironman races are ruined by overfeeding than by underfeeding. Another common reason for athletes not running to their potential is mineral imbalances, usually salt deficiency. This is pretty easy to fix.

My observation in training hundreds of athletes to Ironman races is that many of the athletes who we run past in the races have simply not trained for an Ironman run. You don't need to be running fast, yet I see athletes doing fast-track sessions and neglecting their long endurance runs. Often when they are doing their long endurance run, they're doing it as a race-paced rehearsal. They're not actually going out to condition the muscles to burn fat efficiently.

An endurance run is not a time trial. Leave your Garmin at home; it's not going to help you run faster on race day. The obsession with measuring everything in training has taken the athlete's eye off the ball. The object of the long endurance run is to teach the body to utilize fat more efficiently as a fuel and to condition the muscles in the legs to be out for a long time.

* Try starting the day with a strong espresso brewed from freshly ground beans, not instant coffee. Caffeine kick-starts the body into fat burning mode.

* Start out easy. Endurance, that's efficient fat burning, built at low intensity. A long endurance run is actually run slower than race-day pace.

* Pay attention to good posture and efficient foot placement. The most important thing you can do on race day is hold good posture. We do lots of core-strength work to make sure we can hold good posture. Think about this as you become fatigued. When you're racing everyone around, you are going to be exhausted. Hold yourself together, and you'll creep away from them.

* Shorten your stride on the uphills. You're not here to show anyone how fast you can run up a hill; you're here to work on your efficiency. Make efficiency the goal for the whole run.

* Include short walks to reset the mind back to the best technique and posture. If the thirty-step walks add to the time you're out running but cause you to run more efficiently, you have won on two fronts. The longer you're out there, the more endurance you will build. And if you get used to maintaining great posture through the whole run, it becomes a habit that will reward you on race day.

* Add a walk to the end of your long run to extend the endurance benefits. I usually get home and take the dogs for a twenty- to thirty-minute walk to the park. This extends my endurance and fat burning for another half hour without any more impact on my body.

* Give yourself time to recover from the long run. Make sure you take your antioxidant supplements with your recovery drink. How well you feed after a workout like this will determine how much you gain from it. You'll know if you've done your long run at the right pace if you can come home and mow the lawn after it. You should not be wrecked by it. Slow it down, and enjoy it. Long, slow runs are good for your soul and your longevity in the sport.

Few individuals achieve championship status without a support network of committed people.

The Circle

Life runs in circles; the wheel never stops turning. No matter how dark the night, morning comes. No matter how cold the winter, spring comes.

When you're feeling despair, know that the wheel is turning. Joy will come.

Nature is full of circles. Everywhere we look we can see the circles in action.

If we look closely at elite-level runners, we see the circle being repeated over and over, as the runner flows across the ground. Watch an elite runner's hands as he runs up a hill. His hands are in front of his body, moving in a circular motion and rolling forward as he runs up the hill, with the same leg turnover rate he would use to run along flat ground. Only his stride length has shortened.

As that same runner runs up that hill, look down at his feet. If he had a light on his ankle bone, that light would mark out a series of circles. The runner's foot action is not one of up and down like an ancient winemaker stomping grapes. He moves his feet in a circular motion, lifting up and over the opposite ankle bone, not unlike pedaling a bike. This circular foot placement action is very efficient and is a skill the average runner can learn. Yes, it's possible to learn to be a better runner.

Tiger Woods, Raphael Nadal, Roger Federer, and Pete Jacobs, all have one thing in common, each of these athletes becomes fitter and stronger while practicing perfect technique. Pete is the new breed of Ironman athlete, who is dedicated to "better" rather than "more" practice. Every workout he does has a strong focus on technique. He holds the swim course record on many Ironman courses, but every swim workout is spent perfecting his technique. He often has his stroke videoed so he can analyse and correct tiny inefficiencies. He has run the fastest run split at the last two Hawaii Ironman races, yet every run he does is dedicated to perfecting his run technique.

Good run technique, a good diet, and good body-maintenance procedures prevent injuries. When someone gets a running injury, it's a sign that something is wrong in one or more of those areas.

To perfect running circles, the action must be practiced. The single leg, high-knee drill is the best starting point. Stand on your left foot, hold onto a post or tree with your left hand for stability. Now place your right hand on your right hip (so you know if the pelvis is dipping forward when you cycle the right leg through the running action).

Now with the weight on the left foot, lift the right knee up to a point where the femur is parallel to the ground; the lower leg hangs loose. (Looseness in the lower leg and hip joint is critical.) Now the foot is at the top of the circle.

Move the foot downward to contact the ground with the mid-foot in a sweeping action, accelerating through to the rear and back around to the knee-up position. Be careful to not let the hips rock forward as the foot accelerates through skimming the ground with the mid-foot. Be sure to contact the ground right under the hip. The foot must not strike the ground in front of the hips.

The drill described above is done fast and loose. That's the way fast runners run. It's not only a great way to practice the circular action of the foot placement but also learn to unload muscular tension, which is like a handbrake to a runner. To run faster, you don't try harder; you become looser and more relaxed.

A great way to incorporate this drill into every training run is to run five minutes and then stop for twenty to thirty seconds. Do this drill five times with each leg, and then proceed with the run. If every training run were punctuated like this, the unloading of muscular tension and focus on form would have the athlete finishing long runs fresher and surprisingly having travelled farther.

Standing with even pressure on the ground between the heel and forefoot, now lean forward from the ankles so the ground pressure under the forefoot is up to 60 per cent. This is the forward leaning action that will promote a faster, more efficient running action. The foot travels in a circular motion, not striking the ground but brushing the ground with light contact right under the hips, pushing the ground back. This action has significantly less shock on the body than a heel strike in front of the hips.

It may take a whole winter of practice to own this technique, but it's an investment in both race performance and longevity in the sport.

If there's a champion mindset, it's one that blocks out everything else but the goal or task at hand.

What Do You Think When You Run?

Running is the most basic of all human movements. Swimming and cycling are skills that have to be learned. Humans have been running down their meals since before they began measuring time.

It's such a natural movement it should just happen while we travel from A to B. Triathletes are great at complicating things. Analysis paralysis is an easy affliction to catch. We have heart-rate monitors, GPS watches, and pedometers measuring every step we take.

In long-distance endurance races, controlling what goes on in your head can be the difference between a great race and an unsatisfying experience. The mind will wander if you leave it idle.

What did primitive man think of while he spent long lengths of time chasing an animal. Studies have proven that man is better suited to long endurance events than most of the animals he would have hunted. So it is possible to run down a much faster animal, by working as a team and constantly running the animal to exhaustion. Man is able to dissipate heat much more efficiently than most of his prey.

A primitive man only has one thing on his mind—the process of keeping the animal moving until exhausted. He's not monitoring his heart rate; he's doing that unconsciously by pacing himself. He's smarter than the animal he hunts. He works with other teammates to cut off the animal's escape routes, constantly turning the prey to keep it moving.

Eventually he wins.

What can we learn from our primitive ancestors? First, we are from hunter-gatherer stock. Our ancestors lived on lean meats and vegetables, with a small amount of grain when available. Second, we were born to run, not in shoes with raised heels but barefoot or in thin sandals made from hide. No cushioning, just protection from the prickles.

Third, we are endurance animals. We can turn on a sudden burst of speed when we need it, but it is not sustainable like lower efforts spread over a long duration. Fourth, we would tire quickly if we were calculating how far we've been, how far we have to go, what pace we're travelling at, and what someone else is doing. The primitive hunter had simple thoughts in mind—keep moving, stay loose, and never take your eyes off the prey.

If we could leave our GPS and heart-rate monitors at home on race day and simply stay in the moment (simply do what we have to do to get there as quickly as possible), we could release ourselves of all those controlling thoughts that restrict free movement. We could go faster without trying any more.

Recovering from failure is a most important quality.

Nutrition for Performance

As soon as we bring up the subject of nutrition, many of us instantly think about supplements. Nutrition is food first and supplements second. The purpose of supplements is to work with the best diets we can manage to help make those diets the best they can be.

The mentality of eating whatever we can get our hands on and then fixing it up by taking a handful of pills every morning and night is flawed.

I personally believe anyone training for Ironman distance triathlon—in fact, anyone even training for a marathon—should supplement his or her diet with at least a multivitamin and an oil supplement to ensure enough essential fatty acids.

Dietary supplements will not get you the best training or racing performance unless your basic diet is as good as you can get it.

Most athletes starting on my training plan have not been including enough protein in their diets. My initial review of the their diets often shows why they struggle to stay well or are tired all of the time. Tidying up their diets is often the first positive step on the road to massive PBs.

I'll mention no names, but a young lady who started training with me a couple of years ago was training on a diet based on muffins and coffee. She goes a lot better now on a higher protein intake and a lot of fresh vegetables.

In order to become a good fat burner (have the endurance to race an Ironman well), doing long runs and/or long bikes first thing in the morning without breakfast will encourage the body to search for fuel. This doesn't feel as good as training with a high glycogen level, but it does teach you to burn fat for energy. We wake up each morning with enough fat on board to run or walk for sixty kilometres if we had to. This is even when we're at race weight. Some of the people we see out at the shopping mall have enough fuel stored to hibernate all winter or run or walk for hundreds of kilometres, but their ankles and knees just wouldn't go the distance.

So doing endurance training on an empty stomach will help train your fuel efficiency for the longer races. Carry a few dollars in case you need a Coke to get home.

Now, the opposite is the case on the days you want to train the higher range of your fitness (top end).

On the days when you run a track session, do bike intervals, or do swim speed work, you need to have a high blood sugar level. Start the day with your planned pre-race meal. A liquid meal drink is good. Have an energy replacement drink with you at the track or on the bike. Sip it between efforts.

This strategy will help give you the energy to train harder when you need to train hard. Interval work is of little benefit if you are unable to go hard enough because of low fuel levels. Every workout makes a difference; every good one, that is.

Now, refuelling after training is probably the greatest chance an athlete has to use nutrition to affect his or her race-day performance. Right after training, your body is hungry for sugar. This is when high-glycaemic–index carbohydrates are your friend. A soft drink is both refreshing and full of sugar to refuel your muscles.

Don't stop there. After the soft drink, within forty to fifty minutes of training, have a balanced meal. Balanced means include protein, carbs, and fat. The emphasis should be on carbs (rice, pasta, veges, bread) and then protein next (lean beef, chicken, eggs, fish, nuts). The best fats to include are from vegetables (olive oil, flaxseed oil, avocado, nuts).

Health World produces the best recovery drink I have found on the market. Endura Optimizer is the right balance of carbs and protein to be absorbed quickly and help rebuild energy stores and muscles. Follow this with a balanced meal.

If the goal with every meal is to be high in fresh vegetables (cooked or salad), include fish three to four times per week (canned is okay), and include rice often. Not only is it cheap but also the basis of the Asian diets, which are the healthiest on earth.

Supplements are there to fill in the gaps. If you owned an expensive racehorse, you'd feed him nothing but the best.

The champion mindset—a single-minded focus to block out distractions and just go for it.

Maintaining a Healthy, Strong Immune System

Today I heard a doctor being interviewed on the radio. She reported recent findings pointing to the stronger immune systems in children who attended child-care centres compared to children who stayed at home in more isolated conditions.

Apparently the children exposed to lots of different germs developed a greater resistance to them. Us paranoid athletes who avoid all contact with others just before major races may not be doing ourselves any favours. Fearing illness is a sure-fire way of attracting it into your life.

Last year about this time, our club ran an event called "Cycos Survivor," an all-night event that involved carrying a log for ten kilometres, swimming across Brisbane River twice, travelling through a half-kilometre of storm-water pipes, and running forty-six kilometres. Some observers were shocked at the type of things involved. Swimming in the river and trudging up creek beds and into storm-water tunnels were the types of things we, as kids, did every weekend. We never got sick.

In the past week, I have had contact with two people who have become quite sick after having a flu vaccine. Wouldn't it be better to work on building our immune systems up to full strength so we naturally resist the flu germs? The flu vaccine only protects against one variety of flu. A strong immune system protects us against all types of flu and lots of other illnesses.

Another doctor who was interviewed on the same show a couple of weeks ago stated that 80 per cent of our immunity comes from our stomachs. The millions of bacteria that populate our stomachs are all working together to protect us from attack.

The beneficial bacteria in our stomachs (which is the core of our immunity) can be harmed by poisons on fruit and vegetables, by preservatives in foods, by chlorine in drinking water, by pollutants in the air, and most of all, by antibiotics.

Health starts in the stomach. Every nutrient needed to keep your hair healthy, to keep your skin young and flexible, and to rebuild your muscles so you become stronger from training has to be digested from your food. So your youthful good looks are being maintained by your digestive system collecting enough nutrients from your food to keep repairing your body.

So with the goal of faster swimming, cycling, and running and avoiding illnesses that will prevent us enjoying our passions, we have to watch what goes down our throats.

Harmful chlorine can be absorbed by our skin. How many athletes don't wash their skin with soap after swimming in a chlorinated pool? The chlorine in drinking water can be filtered out. Relatively cheap filters can stop that chlorine getting into your stomach and killing off your little mates.

How many wash fruit and vegetables well enough to get rid of any pesticides? Slight traces of pesticides can harm beneficial bacteria. How many athletes are in doctors' waiting rooms, waiting for another dose of antibiotics for every ailment, which could very likely be avoided by maintaining strong immune systems? The dose of antibiotics is going to further undermine the body's resistance to the next bug that comes along.

Don't get me wrong, antibiotics can save lives. But save them for the life-threatening situations, and then follow them up with a course of Inner Health or one of the other probiotics.

There's lots of controversy about drugs in sport. No one wants to be beaten by someone on performance-enhancing drugs. But put that issue aside for a moment, and go look in your own medicine cupboard. The painkillers, the anti-inflammatory drugs, and a lot of other potions are only necessary because the body is unable to do the job it was designed for. All of these chemical cocktails you faithfully wash down your throat may be harming the immune system designed and tested by nature over the past million years.

I've identified a problem; I should offer an answer.

The healthy athlete's diet should consist of 60 to 70 per cent fresh fruit and vegetables (organic where possible and always well washed). Raw, fresh salads should be eaten often. Some vegetables, cabbage, broccoli, are cauliflower are more easily digested if steamed.

Preserved or smoked meats should be eaten rarely, as a treat maybe. Preservatives in certain foods are designed to stop the natural breakdown of these foods (bacon; ham; corned meat; seafood extender, whatever that is; and processed chicken—you wouldn't want to know what that was made from). What do you think happens when you dump them into your stomach and expect the guys inside to break them down? They do their best, but they die by the millions trying.

Fresh meat and fish are full of nutrients. They also contain important enzymes that will send them "off" in a few hours if left out of the fridge. This enzymatic action is one of the most important chemical reactions in life.

Last year while on holiday in Venice, my wife and I ran out of bottled water in the night and drank tap water. It tasted like it came straight out of the canals. Through the next day, I felt a bit queasy in the stomach, but my wife got quite sick. As the day went on, when we were driving South, she got worse. I seemed okay. I managed to get her some acidophilus capsules from a pharmacy (with great language difficulty). After several doses, she came good over the next twenty-four hours.

We consumed the same amount of water, but I didn't get sick. The difference was that my health guru had given me digestive-enzyme capsules to take at mealtimes, because I couldn't avoid cheese in the standard Italian diet. I have difficulty with dairy foods. I spoke to him when we returned to Brisbane, and he pointed out that digestive enzymes are an important first-line of defence against stomach bugs.

**There are shortcuts to obscurity; but
to success, unfortunately not.**

Eating for Performance and Longevity

Vegetables: Sixty to seventy per cent of your diet should be vegetables—fresh, steamed, and stir-fried.

The best way to get the carbs in your diet necessary for energy to train well is through vegetables. Not only are they supplying the carbs but also fibre (really important for health of the digestive system), vitamins and minerals. Vitamin and mineral supplements are only to fill the gaps in the diet; most of our needs should come from veges.

Protein: Training and working breaks down muscle tissue; protein supplies the raw materials to rebuild it. How well you rebuild your muscle tissue determines how much you gain from training. It's possible to get all your protein from vegetable sources. But you really need to study every meal, and you'll probably die of boredom. Tofu, nuts, beans, and lentils will provide you with all your protein needs. That's what the Dalai Lama eats, but he doesn't often run a marathon after a day in the saddle.

Eating fish three times a week is ideal, but most of us don't. The protein obtained from fish is excellent quality, and any fat it contains is beneficial to our health. The protein available from chicken, beef, pork, and lamb are all of very good quality, but be careful not to consume too much of the fats that come with these products. These are the saturated fats that may lead to many health problems.

Aim to have protein at every meal, about 20 per cent of your total intake is ideal. It can be a little higher in heavy training. Endurance athletes need more protein than body builders. We actually break down more muscle tissue than they do. A cereal breakfast can have its protein content increased by adding a handful of almonds. Raw almonds make an ideal snack to carry, with some dried fruit for those times when you just can't find something decent to eat.

Fats: We need fats to stay healthy. Omega-3 fats found in fish and flax seed oils are dangerously low in the Australian/American diet. We get far too much saturated fat and not enough omega-3 or omega-6 fats. See McDonald's for your saturated fat needs.

Using olive oil for any cooking, using flax-seed oil for salad dressings, and eating avocados regularly will supply us with all the right fats in our diets. A healthy immune system, nervous system, and hormonal system are all dependant on a regular supply of essential fatty acids.

The most dangerous fats are not the saturated fats (from animal sources). The most dangerous fats are the trans fats (the ones man has messed around with like margarine and solidified oils often found in potato chips, corn chips, dips, and so on). These will kill you. See KFC for your trans fat needs.

Don't avoid fat, and don't fear fat; just watch the saturated fats and trans fats (hydrogenated oils).

Grains: Man has remained relatively unchanged for fifty thousand years, living on meat, fish, vegetables, and some grains. In historically recent times (the last two to three hundred years), grains have been cultivated in larger and larger quantities. Whole cultures have been built around wheat and flour consumption. Kellogg's and Quaker Oats (who own Pepsi and Gatorade) have empires built on selling grains to you. They'll dig up all of the supportive research to convince you that you should consume more grain products.

Limit the intake of grains. Favour rice as a carbohydrate source over wheat. Many more humans have trouble digesting wheat than rice.

Dairy foods: Some people thrive on dairy foods. Nestlé has made a fortune out of selling them. Fact is, dairy foods do not suit a huge number of humans. Human milk suits humans (until they grow teeth), not cow milk. Goat-milk products often suit humans better than cow-milk products, but don't tell Nestlé.

Sugar: Early man got his sugar from fruit and honey. Sugar provides energy. Ask anyone who's tried cycling for over four hours on water alone how much he'd pay for a Mars bar. We need sugar for some of our energy needs, especially during long training sessions. Taking in any sort of sugar will get you through an Ironman triathlon or an all-day training session. But consumption of sugar while not training has been responsible for building some huge bodies and causing some terrible health problems.

Don't fear sugar; Coca Cola has made a fortune out of selling it. Just don't consume more than you're going to use as energy. If you don't burn it as energy, you'll most likely store it right where you don't want it.

As endurance athletes, sugar is one of our valuable tools. Take it right after a workout to replenish your glycogen reserves. A can of Coke or another cheap soft drink at the end of a workout rehydrates, refreshes, and sets you up for a better next session.

The healthiest diets in the world are the Mediterranean and Asian diets. These diets usually contain more fish, less meat, and lots of vegetables, and they're very low in dairy foods.

Chocolate: Chocolate is an aphrodisiac, according to research sponsored by Nestlé. Eating chocolate is no problem at all; in fact, eating chocolate is okay, even when you're trying to lose weight. Just eat it early in the day, and exercise after it. If you love chocolate, have a couple of pieces with a black coffee early in the morning, and go out and train for an hour or so. It'll actually help you burn fat.

Coffee: There is nothing wrong with drinking freshly ground coffee; in fact, it actually helps mobilize the stored fats in your body. Drink espresso or long black instead of milk-based coffees if you're trying to lose weight or maintain race weight. The coffee that is not worth drinking is the instant variety. Nestlé

has done well out of this as well. Coffee actually has some health benefits, but only if it's freshly ground and brewed. The oils in coffee degrade shortly after grinding (within hours).

Just don't drink coffee with your meals, as it does interfere with digestion and is best enjoyed away from meals.

Wine: I drink red wine every day and recommend it. It contains antioxidants very beneficial to health and relaxes the stomach prior to eating, aiding in good digestion. Good recovery and longevity are both heavily dependent on good digestion and absorption of nutrients. In Australia we're spoilt with choice and have a huge range of very good wines at reasonable prices. Just lay off the wine in the few days before a major race, as alcohol impairs the liver's ability to store glycogen. I would not have wine for a few days before an Ironman.

High achievers believe in themselves. They have faith in their own capabilities. Their goals and aspirations grow as their capabilities grow.

What's Real?

We're surrounded by fake things. We get so used to fake that we hardly recognise real anymore. My recent trip to Hawaii has reminded me of how much around us is not real.

A walk down the cereal and breakfast-food aisle in the supermarket is a wake-up call. Rows and rows of "food items" that bear no resemblance to the food they once were. In one corner, we found the American version of muesli granola. In the whole aisle, amongst the tons of junk, we found something that would be nutritious enough to bother buying. This is not just America; our breakfast-food departments in Australia are almost as bad.

One item that caught my eye was spray-on cheese. God knows what it actually is. It's packed in a pressure-pack can. You apparently spray it onto sandwiches, nachos, or whatever you're going to eat.

Science has advanced to a stage where Michael Jackson started out a poor black boy and became a rich white man. Science has given us fake smiles, fake breasts, fake fingernails, and many more things that are no longer real. The construction industry has given us fake timber floors, fake rocks, and fake brick.

What worries me is the food industry is focusing too heavily on fake products. Bread that bears no resemblance to the bread my grandparents ate and maple syrup that doesn't come from a maple tree.

Our grandparents ate real food. It came from farms, not factories.

We can choose food from farms. It may not always be that easy, but we can do it if it means we live longer. If it means we stay healthy longer and don't need to be fitted with an artificial heart, artificial hips, or artificial knees.

Human bodies were designed to be nourished with the nutrients digested from fresh foods, either collected, hunted, or grown. Not processed to a point where they bear no resemblance to the original ingredients.

We are smart. We're too smart to be duped by advertising that suggests a product that now costs six times as much per ton, since processing, is nutritionally superior to the original product before processing. How could that be possible? Processing generally degrades the nutritional content of food. It certainly adds to the cost of the food. Just price corn at the produce store, and then compare the price of cornflakes. It's a good business, turning corn into cornflakes. Then add more colours, add more sugar, and maybe change the shapes. The end product bears little resemblance to the original ingredients, and the nutritional benefits are reduced more with every stage of the process.

The people of the world who live longest and have less chronic disease are all living on diets of mainly unprocessed foods—foods from farms, not from factories. Fresh food, live food.

Most people are born with talent, but the majority of people never realise what that talent is.

Oils Ain't Just Oils

We all remember the advertisement for Castrol motor oil, where the mechanic assures the boss he has the best available oil for his car. "Oils ain't oils, Sol!"

Well, it's the same for the oils we use in our own diets. For years I've been advising my athletes to add good oils to their diets to support my theory that you cannot get an unhealthy body fit. To become totally fit, you first have to become totally healthy.

Many of our neighbours and social contacts feel that if they're not sick, then they're healthy. Health is not the absence of illness. Good health is several steps higher than the absence of illness.

Not many of us can train as hard as we'd like and get enough of the important nutrients we need, from our diet without supplementation. I have mentioned earlier what I encourage my athletes to take as supplements. Keep in mind food should come from a farm, not a pill, supplements are simply a back up plan.

When we prepare a salad from farm grown vegetables, we can add a zesty taste to that salad by adding a simple dressing of balsamic vinegar, flax-seed oil, lemon juice, and a little grainy mustard if you like. Shake it, and pour it over your salad. Chopped capers can be added if you like those. The flax-seed oil can be replaced with extra virgin olive oil.

Now, when you're in the supermarket, read the labels of prepared salad dressings. There are a whole lot of extra things added to make it last until you come along and buy it. My salad dressing won't last. It's not designed to last. It's designed to nourish.

If you have fresh herbs available, you can chop these and add them to the dressing. It's truly amazing how easy it is to grow fresh herbs. All you need is a spot where the sun shines for some time each day, a pot or pots, a bag of potting soil, and a few seedlings from the nursery. It's so satisfying to pick your own oregano, basil, coriander, parsley, or rosemary. These are the easiest ones to grow and the ones we use most.

Another way to get good quality oils into the diet is to make a smoothie. The smoothie is an ideal athlete's breakfast (or dinner after evening training). My favourite smoothie recipe is one glass of almond milk, one handful of raw almonds, half a mango, three scoops Endura Optimizer Vanilla, (protein and carbohydrate mixture), one dessert spoon colostrum powder, and two dessert spoons virgin coconut oil. Whip this up, and you have a meal in a cup. Every now and then, I add the contents of an Inner Health capsule for extra probiotics.

The "Sip of Paradise" coconut oil is a delicious oil containing medium chain triglycerides, which are used directly as fuel for the body and not stored as fat. Coconut oil is also available as a tasteless version that can be used in cooking. Coconut oil is very good for cooking because it stands hotter temperatures without breaking down.

Any frying in olive oil needs to be done at lower temperatures (below smoking), as high temperatures destroy the excellent food that it starts out as.

The oils I have listed above—olive, fish, flaxseed, and coconut—are all easier for your body to absorb and turn into energy than sunflower, canola, safflower, and cottonseed oils. The others won't kill you, but they won't get you into the best health you could achieve.

Oils ain't just oils.

I hope my bedtime stories have helped entertain and inform athletes around the world. The idea for this collection came from my own difficulty in reading more than two or three pages of whichever book I was reading, before falling asleep. One of the benefits of this great life we've discovered, is we have no trouble sleeping.

After more than thirty years in this sport, I've met hundreds of great people, and had the chance to change the lives of hundreds. People come into your life to either teach you something, or to learn something from you. When an athlete moves on to whatever they choose after a period under my instruction, I hope they move on healthier and better informed than when they came into my life.

Train safe, enjoy the journey.

Al

*** Please visit http://www.aptriathlon.com/ ****

Milton Keynes UK
Ingram Content Group UK Ltd.
UKHW011258051223
433834UK00001B/132